2 i Cataloghi dell' Accademia
di architettura

Aurelio Galfetti
Director of the Academy of Architecture
of the Italian Language Swiss University

The Academy of Architecture of the Italian Language Swiss University organizes two exhibitions a year at the Art Museum of Mendrisio, alternating between the presentation of contemporary architects and a review of the great masters of our century.

These exhibitions are complemented by a bilingual catalogue produced in cooperation with the prestigious Skira publishing house. This book, although primarily intended for students enrolled in Swiss and Italian schools of architecture, can also be found in general circulation.

After the exhibition on the Parisian architect Patrick Berger and the present one dedicated to the construction, by Louis I. Kahn, of the Kimbell Art Museum in Fort Worth, the next exposition will show works by the Portuguese architect Eduardo Souto de Moura. We hope the Kimbell Art Museum may prove very useful to students, as well as to anyone who wishes to investigate its distinctive features, and to gain some insight into the long and arduous quest that often characterizes a creative process — even that of a great master such as Louis I. Kahn.

The design of the Kimbell Art Museum is the product of extraordinary intuition, and results in a masterly synthesis that solves all the problems posed by the site and by the specific purpose of the construction.

The works of Louis I. Kahn have already been exhibited in Europe on other occasions, but the Academy considered the selection of a single building to be more interesting, and presents it in detail and in a didactical fashion — a fitting approach for a school which aims to shape architects who are professional figures able to keep a subtle balance between theory and practice.

Louis I. Kahn

The Construction
of the Kimbell Art Museum

With
the financial support
of
Banca dello Stato
del Cantone Ticino

Design and organization
of the exhibition and catalogue

Luca Bellinelli

Organization at the Art Museum

Luca Bellinelli
Aurelio Galfetti

Archive material for the exhibition
and catalogue

Louis I. Kahn Collection,
The Architectural Archives
of the University of Pennsylvania,
Philadelphia;
The Kimbell Art Museum Archives
in Fort Worth, Texas;
Marshall D. Meyers
Pasadena, California

Translation

Patricia Ranzi–Gedey

Graphic design

Bruno Monguzzi
Alberto Bianda

Layout

Studio grafico
Dal Ben–Steiger Felder

Publisher

Skira editore

Cover picture

North courtyard with Maillol "L'aire",
looking north

This catalogue was issued on the
occasion of the exhibition dedicated
to the construction of the Kimbell
Art Museum in Forth Worth
by architect Louis I. Kahn. The
publishing activities are a function
of the Istituto di documentazione
of the Architecture Academy
of Mendrisio which, together
with the Library and the Archives,
complement the didactical
activities of the School.

Special thanks go to Dr. Patricia
Cummings Loud, the curator
of architecture of the Kimbell Art
Museum, to Julia Moore Converse,
the director of the Architectural
Archives at the University
of Pennsylvania in Philadelphia,
together with architect William
Whitaker, as well as to the architect
Marshall D. Meyers, Louis Kahn's
project architect for the Kimbell
Museum and other works; and to the
photographer Michael Bodycomb for
their support and guidance during
the research process. They have
provided precious archive material
and unpublished documents,
both historical and contemporary.
Their unfailing helpfulness and
receptiveness were invaluable.

First published in Italy in 1999
by Skira editore S.p.A.
Palazzo Casati Stampa
via Torino 61, 20123 Milano, Italy

© 1997, © 1999
by Accademia di architettura
dell'Università della Svizzera
italiana, Mendrisio,
for texts and illustrations
© 1997, © 1999
by Skira editore, Milan

Printed and bound in Italy.
First edition
ISBN 88-8118-471-0

Distributed in North America
and Latin America by Abbeville
Publishing Group, 22 Cortlandt
Street, New York, NY 10007, USA.
Distributed elsewhere in the world
by Thames and Hudson Ltd.,
181a High Holborn, London
WC1V 7QX, United Kingdom.

Table of Contents

Preface

Luca Bellinelli

[1] Joseph Rykwert, "Louis I. Kahn: An Introduction", p. 10 of the catalogue.
[2] Vittorio Gregotti, "Modern Connection", in *Rassegna, Louis I. Kahn 1901/1974*.
[3] Louis I. Kahn, Conference held on 14 November 1967 at the New England Conservatory, "Architecture d'aujourd'hui", N. 142, 1969.

The Kimbell Museum is one of the most "modest and unpretentious[1]" constructions by Louis I. Kahn. In spite or possibly because of this, and because of its cozy, intimate feel, it is also one of his most remarkable achievements.

There are at least two reasons why this is so. One concerns the emblematic character and design, two aspects which are always closely associated in Kahn's work. The representativeness of the work as a public building, the powerful statement of its constitutive elements, and its design, which is strongly connected to the constructional aspects[2] [...] in every respect the Kimbell Art Museum, more than any other of Kahn's buildings, expresses the architect's habitual concern that "a room must be designed for its light". Light was indeed the dominant theme. It was a determinant factor, not only for Kahn, but to even a greater extent for Richard Brown, who was already director of the Kimbell before its construction, as well as in the early period of its activity.

Referring to the "museum in Texas" he was designing, Kahn said: "Here I felt that the light in the rooms structured in concrete will have the luminosity of silver. [...] The scheme of enclosure of the museum is a succession of cycloid vaults [...] each forming the rooms with a narrow slit to the sky, with a mirrored glass shaped to spread natural light on the sides of the vault. This light will give a touch of silver to the room [...]. Added to the skylight from the slit over the exhibit rooms, I cut across the vaults, at a right angle, a counterpoint of courts, open to the sky, of calculated dimensions and character..."[3] Kahn was already so concerned with light during the initial stages of the design that his first sketches, those of spring 1967 (he had been first approached about the project in April of the preceding year, which allowed him ample time for reflection) are not dedicated to the size of the building or its organization, but to light, its infiltration from above, and reflection down the walls, breathing life into the works of art and conveying to visitors that "comforting feeling of knowing the time of day."

Further reasons which make the Kimbell Art Museum particularly interesting go back to the story behind the project and the practical aspects of the construction. Louis I. Kahn had to work with a local firm which was to take care of the construction plans and on site inspections. However, this cooperation did not run smoothly. The relationship between the architects (Louis I. Kahn and Preston M. Geren) became strained, as their manners of defining the design stage were diametrically opposed. Geren believed the design stage should end as soon as work on the construction plans began, whereas Louis I. Kahn had a tendency to prolong the time for research even into the construction stage, his obvious aspiration being that of finding, even at the last moment, some constructive detail or spatial solution which would allow a breakthrough in the design itself. The presence of valuable assistants, in particular Marshall D. Meyers, allowed Louis I. Kahn to overcome misunderstandings, and the new Kimbell Art Museum to become, in a very short time, one of the major architectural works of the last twenty-five years.

This catalogue and the exhibition which is its raison d'être aim to be just a modest illustration of the theoretical and practical implications in the design of the Kimbell Art Museum by Louis I. Kahn. We have tried to document a broad outline of his research from the original idea—the power that light represents—to the construction drawings with a study—albeit inevitably reduced—of the intermediary stages during which the project underwent constant alterations, both by the architect and by the client, Ric Brown, until two years later the final plan was developed for the museum that was to become a reference point in twentieth-century architecture.

This undertaking of ours has greatly benefited from the support of prominent personalities in the Kimbell history such as Marshall D. Meyers, the competent and most solicitous project architect of the Kimbell Art Museum; Patricia Cummings Loud, into whose care the architectural work has been entrusted, and whose expertise is recognized in this and other fields; and Professor Joseph Ryckwert, an authority in art history, who now holds the chair that used to be Louis I. Kahn's at the University of Pennsylvania in Philadelphia.

The story of the Kimbell Art Museum is commendable in the way it has developed from an original idea, reminding us of the cultural postulates into which we hope the figure of the architect will increasingly take root. It is a figure which draws inspiration from an association with other disciplines, but which, at all times, should be able to ensure the centrality of an architectural project.

Louis Kahn: An Introduction

Joseph Rykwert

Born in Warsaw, Joseph Rykwert studied in England, and taught at the Royal College of Art in London, as well as at Essex and Cambridge Universities. He is director of the Ph D program for architecture at the University of Pennsylvania in Philadelphia and the author of many books, among which: *On Adam's House in Paradise*, *The Idea of a Town*, *The Brothers Adam*, *The First Moderns* and *The Necessity of Artifice*. Many of his publications have been translated into Italian.

1.
Paul Philippe Cret, Detroit Institute of Art, 1922–1927
2.
"Ecole Nationale de Beaux-Arts", Paris. Atelier in the 1930's
3.
Louis I. Kahn, Saint Peter's Square, Rome
4.
George Howe and William Lescaze, skyscraper of the Philadelphia Savings Fund Society, Philadelphia, 1932

Louis Kahn was a late developer. Giuseppe Terragni, who was three years younger, was dead before Kahn did the first work that made him famous. Alvar Aalto, who was only three or four year his senior, had already done some of his most important buildings before World War II.

Once his particular approach to architecture had matured however, and he had made himself independent, his way forward was astonishingly rapid and secure. The security came—in part—from his attachment to the city in which he had grown up and studied, Philadelphia. He was four when he arrived in the USA (he was born in Estonia), so that English was his natural language. School was in Philadelphia, and he was also trained as an architect at the University of Pennsylvania there. One of his teachers was Paul Philippe Cret, who had, for his part, arrived in Philadelphia from Paris in 1903.

Most American architects of note had passed through some form of Beaux-Arts training—whether in France or in one of the schools and ateliers offering French-derived training in the USA. But Cret had brought with him a revisionist approach to the Parisian training, as he had been a star pupil in one of the more "advanced" Paris ateliers of the Ecole des Beaux-Arts, and his teaching was therefore surprisingly free of the historicism prevalent in American schools. He concentrated on the virtues of the plan as the generating form, on the power of proportion, on humility before the builder's task. Kahn became more than a pupil of Cret's: he became a disciple and a collaborator. Soon after he graduated, he went on his European "grand tour" and on his return, in 1929, was engaged by Cret to work on his most famous project, the Folger Shakespeare Library in Washington.

Since the Beaux-Arts influence on Kahn is often invoked, it is important to remember that he approached it through Cret's version of it as a rational, almost a scientific procedure, as a method of analyzing the program to translate it into a plan from which the volumes of the building are in turn developed—rather than as a stylistic or decorative training. When—soon after World War II—the young Holmes Perkins arrived at the University of Pennsylvania as their new dean from Harvard, he realized that the Philadelphia experience was not welcoming to the anti-historical, somewhat antiseptic doctrine taught at Gropius-dependent schools. Kahn's more subtle but—in some ways—even harsher teaching became central to the way the school was to proceed. And his memorable dicta (even if sometimes rather gnomic) came to be associated with the "Philadelphia School."

But that was after 1950. Through the depression years Kahn had had a somewhat thin time. There was not a great deal of work in the early thirties, but in 1937 he was able to establish his own office. Much of the work that came his way then was low-cost housing; in tandem with that he also began doing research on urban planning problems, mostly in the context of Philadelphia.

In that connection he met and then worked with George Howe, who is now mostly remembered as the co-author (with William Lescaze) of the Pennsylvania Savings Fund Society building (the first 33-story "modern" skyscraper) as well as with Oskar Stonorov, a Swiss-trained German architect who had emigrated to the USA towards the end of the twenties and had also settled in Philadelphia.

Of course that earlier work was good, but it was not surprising. Kahn did a great deal of housing, both low- and high-rise for local authorities. Had he died at fifty, he would have remained a footnote in the

1.

2.

3.

4.

9.

10.

history of twentieth-century architecture. It was not until 1950, when he designed the art gallery at Yale, that his colleagues were alerted and became aware that a new and startling figure had appeared. For all its rather tame fenestration and plain wall treatment, this relatively small building is very innovative in its use of a complex floor slab composed of three-dimensional elements, which even included a lighting and ventilation system; more unusual was the clear, harshly geometrical articulation of the interior. It was that articulation which aroused immediate curiosity and even enthusiasm about the Yale Gallery. The Yale building had come his way as a result of agitation by George Howe, who became dean of the school of architecture there in 1950 and who had a very high opinion of Kahn's work. Almost immediately after, the Jewish community at Trenton, New Jersey, commissioned a bath house as part of a much larger project for a community center. The cruciform Bath House reiterates the harsh geometries: four thirty-foot square pavilions (each roofed by a slate pyramid) surround a square, thirty-foot open court; they are articulated by eight-foot square, hollow columns which house the element serving the pavilions: that distinction between served and serving areas, which he first made in Trenton, became very important to Kahn. He even commented once that when he had realized it, he considered himself truly independent. Of the large projected Trenton community center only one other small and poor fragment was built. However the approach Kahn developed in this project determined the volumes of his first major building, the one that finally established his international reputation: the Richards Medical Center at the University of Pennsylvania in Philadelphia.

The sad story of that building (of its working deficiencies and its maltreatment by its users) is all too familiar. Nevertheless, the soar

ing duct-tower, the articulation of the floorplanes, the rhythm of the windows, the cunning use of brick and precast concrete (some of it due to his engineer, Auguste Komandant) were memorable. In spite of the University of Pennsylvania, which gave Kahn no further commissions, the building soon became a pilgrimage center for architects from all over the world.

Although during the decade 1947–1957 Kahn spent some time teaching at the Yale school (where he was also building the gallery), Philadelphia was his home and remained his academic base until he died. It is even said that when a president of Harvard was trying to woo him away and he was raising his demands (all of which the president was willing to satisfy), Kahn finally defeated the exercise by saying: "And tell me, President X, what is a Philadelphian going to do in Cambridge, Massachusetts?" But Philadelphia, which is not kind to its sons (witness the early film-comedian W.C. Fields' constant jibes at his home town: he wanted "I would even rather be in Philadelphia" inscribed on his tombstone), occupied him constantly. While his plans for its development during and immediately after World War II remain relatively conventional (and include his largest executed Philadelphia scheme, the Mill Creek housing project), in the nineteen-fifties he devoted a great deal of creative energy to city planning, and his proposals were as startling and as assured as his architecture of the same period. These include some of his most adventurous projects: the tetrahedral high-rise building and the Civic Forum (which Philadelphia did not have nor was destined to have), the traffic zoning with its river-and-canal metaphor and its "harbors"—the car silo towers—that others have often copied though they have never been applied in a real situation.

The tetrahedral buildings are associated with Kahn's assistant at

5.

6.

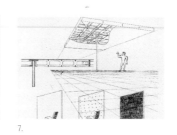

7.

8.

11.

12.

the time, Anne Tyng, and her interest in Buckminster Fuller's space-structures. However, the possibilities of combining three-dimensional elements into slabs and into structures at an urban scale were being explored by a number of engineers at the time. One of the most distinguished was the Frenchman Robert Le Ricolais; his work has been rather neglected lately, though I well remember the excitement the early publication (in 1947) by Techniques et Architecture caused. Le Ricolais was invited to the University of Pennsylvania at that time and conducted a prolific experimental structure laboratory there. Kahn and Le Ricolais became good friends and constant drinking companions.

As his fame grew, Kahn's studio attracted an international group of students: American, of course, but also English, French, Italian, German, Indian, Japanese. What was remarkable about his atelier crits (one of his most brilliant students, Christian Devillers, once told me) was that he avoided making negative criticisms of his pupils' work, so that the whole atelier could sense the quality of a project by the amount of time Kahn spent searching for the positive thing to say about it.

At the University of Pennsylvania, he was the first holder of the Paul Philippe Cret chair, founded to commemorate his mentor (of which I am his unworthy successor). But, for all his acknowledged debt to Cret, and his passionate interest in the past of architecture, Kahn's work cannot be considered either "historicist" (in the sense in which it has been used in association with "postmodernism" or even "Beaux-Arts." Historical references (to Roman architecture for instance—he particularly admired Hadrian's Villa and the Pantheon—or to medieval castles) were digested by him and always became internal to the project—they were never explicit. His passionate concern with materials, their nature and their use, became

he touchstone of his theory and his teaching.
He is known to have exhorted his pupils repeatedly to think about what the particular brick or concrete beam "wanted to be"—which is as unacademic a sentiment as is possible.

The essential modernity of his approach is important for another reason: practically all his buildings since the beginning of the nineteen-fifties, during the quarter-century of his independent activity, were for institutions: he designed churches and synagogues, academic (including museums), civic, government, even commemorative buildings. Little housing, fewer and fewer private houses. That aspect of his work motivated him. The business of architecture is always (or so he thought) concerned with making society conscious of its own structures: "One of the most important aids in the work that I do comes from the realization that any building belongs to some institution of man," he once said. Of course this is also true of private houses, but in Kahn's work it is the public face of the building, its declaratory power, which will strike any observer and which will be evident even in the most modest and retiring of his buildings like the Kimbell Museum.

Kahn's consistent preoccupation with the public function of architecture, his hieratic organization of volume, his uncanny ability to control the entry of light into the spaces be designed and his stern moralism about the use of materials set him at odds with his contemporaries and with the generations which followed him, but they also make him one of the great figures of the twentieth century.

13.

14.

15.

16.

Louis I. Kahn's Kimbell Art Museum

Patricia Cummings Loud

Patricia Cummings Loud obtained degrees in Art History from Radcliffe College and Harvard. She is presently curator of architecture at the Kimbell Art Museum and is a well-known scholar of the work of Louis I. Kahn, her specialty being the museums designed by this Philadelphia architect. She lectures in the United States and abroad, and has taught at Brown University, as well as at the University of Connecticut and the Texas Christian University. Her books *In Pursuit of Quality, the Kimbell Art Museum* (Fort Worth 1986), and *The Art Museums of Louis I. Kahn* (Durham and London 1989) are widely known.

1.
Ground-breaking Mrs. Velma Kimbell, June 27, 1969
2.
Ground-breaking Reception -
The building's model arouses interest, June 27, 1969
3.
Site plan of the area that also hosts the Amon Center Museum and the Modern Art Museum of Fort Worth
4.
Aerial view of the Kimbell Art Museum

This exhibition dedicated to Kahn's Kimbell Art Museum in the fall of 1997 has particular significance. It is an event commemorating a special building held by many in great esteem. It also commemorates a distinguished architect, for whom it was the last work completed during his lifetime. It coincides with the twenty-fifth anniversary of the opening of the museum to the public in October 1972. Such are the facts recognized by the organization of the exhibition. But Louis Kahn was renowned as teacher, not only as an architect. So it is fitting that this exhibit gives students of architecture the opportunity of becoming more familiar with the qualities of this remarkable structure—at once both old and new, simple and intricate, austere and beautiful—and of becoming aware of the complexities of its design and construction.

The Kimbell Art Museum is a public art museum for the exhibition, interpretation, and preservation of works of art of the highest aesthetic quality derived from all periods and cultures in the history of humankind and in any medium or style. The art it collects is general and comes in principle from all time and places, but the actual domain is shared by its near neighbors: the Amon Carter Museum collects and shows American art; the Fort Worth Museum of Modern Art concentrates on contemporary art.

The Kimbell building contain 120,000 square feet (11,150 square meters) and is located in a park of 9.5 acres about two miles (3.26 kilometers) from the center of Fort Worth, Texas. It consists of six-teen parallel, 100 x 20-foot (approximately 30.5 x 6 meters), lead-roofed vaults of architectural concrete, cast in place. These are massed as tripartite units of six, four, and six, separated by two sections, each three feet wide (about 92 cm). Each vault is supported on four corner columns, each of these two square feet. Three open porticoes on the west form the museum's principal facade. A glass wall with doors is sheltered under the recessed center portico behind a forecourt of yaupon hollies-growing in formal, regular rows; the other two porches are fronted by reflecting pools with spilling fountains. The approaches to this facade are from streets to the north and south of the site: paths lead to the porticoes, and there are possible routes around the pools on classical walkways of crushed stones. We walk on gravel under the grove of hollies before climbing low steps up to the entrance portico.

More than one sense is aroused by this approach. We hear the splash of falling water, the crunch of small stones and the echo of firm surfaces underfoot; we see and feel warm sunlight and cool shadow as we stroll along the paths, beside the pools, and under porches and small trees. Around the museum there are landscaped "green rooms," pleasant outdoor courts for sculpture, a pool, gardens, trees, or car parks (some of these are sunken, some slightly raised) and a wide, grassy lawn.

Both the owner, the Kimbell Art Foundation, a private foundation dedicated to the museum, and the client, museum director Richard

1.

2.

3.

4.

5. 6.
Exterior view of the building: lateral
façades, front porticos
7. 8.
Trees facing the main entrance

F. Brown, wanted a building that was a work of art in itself and that attained the high aesthetic standards of the collections. They wanted a special ambiance in the building, to enhance as effectively and as pleasantly as possible the experience of art. This was a new museum, its collections still in the process of formation. It offered an opportunity to strive for ideal viewing conditions. The visitor was meant to be completely absorbed, without distraction, in the contemplation of objects. At the same time the architect was asked to provide all the supportive facilities, space, and equipment needed for the care and interpretation of the collections. Daylight in the galleries was requested at a time when controlled artificial light was the norm in contemporary museums. It was believed by the owner and the client to be the best possible light for viewing works of art, especially those older works, themselves created under such conditions, that the Foundation was collecting. Variable natural light would connect the visitor to objects like these, as would also the introduction into the building of elements of nature—foliage, sky, sun, water. A sense of the seasons and an awareness of the weather would relate the world of the present to the world of the past by illustrating that certain realities from then and now are much the same. As a parallel, great works of art also endure through time. Most people the building was to serve, according to Richard Brown, would not be art professionals of any kind. In his words, they were not expected to be "art historians, other architects, or progressive artists with a sophisticated background of architectural form. Their total experience of a visit to the museum should be one of warmth,

mellowness and even elegance [...] The spaces, forms and textures should maintain a harmonious simplicity and human proportion between visitor and the building and the art objects observed."

Architect Louis Kahn found these requirements to be inspiring. He, too, believed in the need for natural light in a building. "Structure," he said in the 1972 address he gave on the occasion when Gold Medal award was conferred on him by the American Institute of Architects, "is the giver of light," the two together endow the room with "its character, its spiritual aura." Kahn envisioned a museum with "the luminosity of silver," illuminated by "natural light, the only acceptable light for a work of art, [with] all the moods of an individual day." He achieved this through a design with "narrow slits to the sky" to admit daylight and pierced-metal reflectors ("natural light fixtures," he called these) hanging beneath them to diffuse and spread the light onto the underside of cycloid-shaped vaults and on down the walls. Courtyards, lunettes, and light slots introduce more light, varying quality and intensity. Architectural space and light appear blended, an effect enhanced through the employment of deftly handled structural concrete, juxtaposed with Italian travertine, fine-grained white oak, dull-finished metal, and clear glass. Visual serenity is the result.

On the upper level are the public spaces of galleries, courts, restaurant, auditorium, bookstore, and, for museum staff, a library with a mezzanine. With their lighting from different sources—skylights,

5.
6.
7.
8.

11.

12.

9. 10. 11. 12.
Details of the formwork pattern, the combination of different materials, and the treatment of the surfaces
13. 14. 15. 16.
The interior courtyards are characterized by their different color of light, which is then reflected into the exhibition halls

courtyards, lunettes—all these share in a perception of light and space as one. On the lower level there is a single public lobby doubling as a gallery, together with a divided stairway rising to the upper floor and an entrance from the parking court on the east. That level contains museum offices, conservation laboratory, photography studio and darkroom, workshops, storage, and a truck dock. Except for the photography and storage areas, natural light is also important here. These spaces have their own courtyard, light wells and window slots, although they lack the ethereal light from above.

Its architect characterized the museum building as being inspired by "Roman greatness," and, indeed, the classical appearance of its porticoes, arches, and vaults is often cited. Early in the design process Kahn even predicted that the effect of the future museum would be close to that of a Pompeian house with its courtyards. The building's forms, however, while appearing ancient, were achieved using advanced contemporary construction techniques for shell roofs and modern reinforced, post-tensioned concrete, all calculated by structural engineer August E. Komendant. Rome knew no such techniques. Warm, gray concrete, the glass, the brushed aluminum, and the milled steel that some might consider industrial materials—these are used alongside the traditional, creamy-colored travertine and quarter-sawn white oak, as well as the leaden, metallic roofing. For Kahn they were all "natural" and therefore visually related.

There is no obvious ornamentation, only the simple, plain surfaces

of the materials themselves and forms that seem purified as well as simplified. That is why I have characterized this building as at once both old and new, simple and complex, austere and beautiful.

Since 1972 recognition of the Kimbell Art Museum's architecture and collections has only increased. Richard Brown, as client, emphasized the desired qualities in a museum for the public over attributes that might appeal more specifically to "art historians, other architects, [and] progressive artists with a sophisticated background. "His request might have been seen as catering to popular taste, but in the end it led to a building that is a professional success. As he placed the first works in the museum collection into the completed galleries, Brown remarked with elation, "This is what every museum man has been looking for ever since museums come into existence: an uninterrupted floor, perfect lighting, total freedom and flexibility to use the space and install art exactly the way you want." The test of time has proven the building. This design shows itself to be quite functional, flexibly adapting to changing arrangements for varying exhibitions because of its movable wall panels. Its light and atmosphere of serenity are widely acknowledged to enhance the appreciation of works of art seen within its galleries. Art specialists, architects, and artists have joined ordinary visitors in honoring Kahn's achievements. The museum is, as it was intended to be, a work of art that does not dominate but rather enriches the contemplation of the objects it contains. Again, in the words of Louis Kahn, it is "an offering to architecture."

13.

14.

15.

16.

Making the Kimbell: A Brief Memoir

Marshall D. Meyers

Master of Architecture, Yale University, 1957. Editor-in-Chief, *Perspecta 4*, the Yale Architectural Journal, 1957. Fellow of AIA, 1994. Office of Louis I. Kahn, 1957–1973, major projects: Project Architect, Kimbell Art Museum, Fort Worth, Texas; Baltimore Inner Harbor Project, Baltimore, Maryland; Memorial to the Six Million Jewish Martyrs, Battery Park, New York City; Salk Institute for Biological Studies, La Jolla, California; A.N. Richards Medical Research Laboratory, University of Pennsylvania, Philadelphia, Pennsylvania. Completed the Design and Construction of the Yale Center for British Art after the death of Louis I. Kahn, 1974-1977. National Honor of the American Institute of Architects for Excellence in Design for the completion of the Yale Center for British Art, 1978. Lecturer and teacher at Yale University, University of Pennsylvania, Montana State University, Drexel University, Rensselaer Polytechnic Institute, University of California at Los Angeles. Articles published in numerous architectural publications.

1.
Site model to a scale of 1:1200
(Kimbell Art Museum)
2.
Model for the first version of the
project or "Square-plan," spring 1967
(Kimbell Art Museum)
3.
Model for the second version
of the project or "H-plan," fall 1967
(Kimbell Art Museum)
4.
Model for the third version of the project or
"C-plan," fall 1968 (Kimbell Art Museum)

About 2:00 a.m., November 30, 1967

It was night. The gentle drone of the aircraft helped me sleep. Abruptly the pilot banked to the right and I was startled awake. Peering out the window I caught a glimpse of the scattered lights of the Texas countryside below and realized we were on our approach to Love Field. The white-haired man next to me was still sound asleep. After all, we had both been up for days. Being "en charrette" it's called, a term bequeathed from the Ecole Des Beaux-Arts at a time when architecture students would put their drawings into a cart (une charrette) to be hauled away to their professor's house for evaluation. If the drawings were incomplete, the students would hop into the cart with them and keep working. Today there are no carts. But the term persists. It's what architects do when there are deadlines ahead and more work to do than time allows.

This was to be the big presentation. Now the moment of truth was here and we would learn whether the client would accept, even be enthusiastic about, this latest scheme for a small museum in Fort Worth.

The man next to me woke up, rubbed his eyes, and asked if we were there. "Almost," I said. "We are making our descent."

One Month Earlier

I had been away from Lou Kahn's office for two years and had returned to work on the Kimbell Art Museum project. As was usual for Kahn, he was behind schedule. He had signed the contract for the Kimbell project on October 5, 1966, and since that time had only made two presentations to the client, one in March of 1967 and another in June of the same year. These presentations were very sketchy and consisted of models and drawings showing a variety of roof forms, some angled, some semi-circular, and an assortment of reflecting devices suspended under an aperture in the roof. The Director of this new museum, Richard Fargo Brown (known fondly as "Ric" Brown), thought that he should let Kahn work without pressuring him so as not to inhibit the creative spirit.

In those early sketches and models, Kahn had conceived of the museum as a series elements consisting of long narrow galleries, each with its own moveable walls, source of daylight, conditioned air, and electric lighting, a concept that would remain through all of the permutations to come.

Kahn often would talk about "What to do" and "How to do it." The "What to do" was what Kahn referred to as "Form," the realization

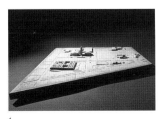

1.

2.

3.

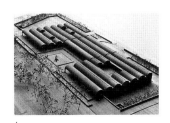

4.

that, if confirmed by consensus, would be the essence of the work and in truth would not belong to him. The "How to do it" was "Design," that which would respond to the circumstance of the program, site, technology, and, most importantly, the art of the architect, and that would belong to him. He would tell us that "spoon" meant a bowl and a handle. But "a spoon" meant a spoon created by Cellini. For Kahn, then, the form-concept of the museum remained unchanged. The permutations were his development of the design.

Brown liked the initial schemes but he felt that the shape of the roofs made the space too lofty. He wanted the museum to have the sense of a large house or villa and not that of a palace, which he felt was too intimidating. So, as Kahn's Project Architect, the task fell to me to find a way to make a lower roof shape. I tried several variations and in one early sketch I hit on the idea of making the daylight reflector both reflect and transmit light, what in the field of optics is called a "beam splitter." I got the idea from a 16mm movie camera I owned, which had a partially mirrored prism which directed a small amount of light to the eyepiece and the rest to the film. The camera was a Bolex made in Switzerland and it inspired a most important feature of the Kimbell, a building we honor 25 years later in that same country.
Kahn was intrigued by this idea and called it a "new kind of window"

when he showed it to Brown. How we found a new shape for the roof was left to chance. I remember I was at home on a Sunday and for no obvious conscious reason, I took a book from my bookshelf titled *Surface Structures in Building* by Fred Angerer. It was a book about shell construction, originally from Germany, now translated into English and printed in Great Britain. I thumbed through the book and on page 43 I saw line drawings illustrating four types of cross-sectional curves for barrel shells: semi-circle, ellipse, cycloid, and sector of a circle. Though the cycloid was unfamiliar, I was struck by the grace of this curve and saw that it perhaps could fulfill our needs. When I showed it to Kahn he accepted it without hesitation and we began to prepare section drawings. I called our local Structural Engineer, Nicholas Gianopolos, to discuss the feasibility of the cycloid structure, but when he learned that we intended to cut out a slot at the top of the curve for the skylight, he told me that we had effectively destroyed the integrity of the shell and that analysis of this was beyond his expertise. "Call Gus," he said. "Gus" was Dr. August Komendant, an expert on concrete structures who had engineered an early Kahn project, and the first project I worked on for Kahn, the Richards Medical Research Building at the University of Pennsylvania. That structure was built of precast, pre- and post-tensioned reinforced concrete, an innovation for a seven story laboratory in the United States. We arranged to see Komendant, who lived

5.

6.

7.

8.

about two hours away in Upper Montclair, New Jersey.

I gathered up our drawings and drove with Mike Brenner, another architect in the office, to see Komendant. It was a gray day and the trip north from Philadelphia was uneventful. Komendant greeted us, puffing on his perpetual pipe, and looked at our drawings. Then he opened a large German book, pointed to a drawing of a cycloid and, in his abrupt manner of speaking just said "yup" (translated "yes"). And he confirmed that the shell could be only four inches thick (we had intuitively drawn it that way) and he added upright curbs on either side of the skylight opening. He also added what he called a "diaphragm" of concrete at the open ends of the cycloid, two feet thick and a constant one foot deep which followed the contour of cycloid.

Development of the reflector proceeded intuitively. In the short month we had before the November 30th presentation, I made sample shapes of the reflector out of plexiglas to a scale of 1/2"=1'-0" (1:24) and a factory in New Jersey deposited a light coating of aluminum on them in a vacuum chamber. At the same time we constructed a wood model of two cycloid bays to the same scale. When we suspended one of the plastic reflectors in the model, and directed a light from above, we saw that the idea worked. Light passed through the reflector and simultaneously cast a soft glow onto the underside of the cycloid.

On the night of November 29th, 1967, armed with the wood model, large colored elevation and section drawings, and plans, Louis Kahn and I took off from Philadelphia airport and headed for Texas.

About 4:00 a.m., November 30, 1967

One image seen on our drive from Dallas to Fort Worth that early morning is still lodged in my memory: the distant view across the flat landscape of tall buildings outlined in colored lights against the dark sky. In 25 days it would be Christmas and Fort Worth traditionally lighted the edges of its skyscrapers this way to celebrate the holiday season. I had never seen such a sight before. Still groggy from lack of sleep and perhaps a bit naively, I believed it to be the symbol of a city that would be open to new ideas.

Later That Morning

The meeting was a success. Ric Brown and the Board of Directors approved the scheme unanimously. Peter Plagens, writing for *Artforum Magazine*, reported on it in the February 1968 issue. Yet ahead lay five years of work, crises, successes, and near failures, before everyone's hope was fulfilled.

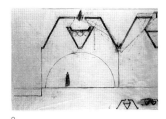

9.

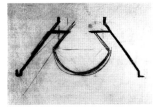

10.

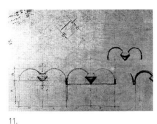

11.

12.

Winter, 1967–68, An Aesthetic Crisis

At that first meeting with Komendant in November of 1967, he told us that the end diaphragm would be uniformly one foot high in elevation and the drawings and the wood model presented to the client on November 30th indicated this. In those drawings, Kahn had placed a narrow, cast glass "lunette" window between the top of the stone infill wall and the underside of the structural concrete diaphragm. This was intended to clearly show that the concrete structure was not supported by the stone infill wall. All was harmonious because the diaphragm, the lunette window, and the top of the infill wall all followed the profile of the cycloid. But soon after, Komendant revised this decision. He now designed the diaphragm with a profile that, in elevation, was deeper at the center of the cycloid and narrower at the ends of the cycloid. He did this, he said, to allow for the required transverse post-tensioning strands in the diaphragm and that it would be the correct expression for this condition. He even went so far as to say that he never told us that the diaphragm was to have a constant section. This was confusing, but more importantly to Kahn, this absolute expression of a minor structural condition was not his inclination. He preferred to express the more general aspect of a structural member rather than every nuance. As an example, he would design cantilevered concrete beams with a constant height for their full length rather than reduce the beam's section the farther it cantilevered.

It was gray, chilly, and damp on the winter day when three of us went to appeal to Komendant to change his mind. Kahn took reinforcements: Carlos Vallhonrat (also from his office) and me. It was to be three against one. But Komendant wouldn't budge. Most of that afternoon Kahn and Komendant drank Aquavit, Komendant puffed on his pipe, and each told stories about his boyhood. And the diaphragm stayed the way Komendant designed it.

Once back in his office, Kahn showed me how he would meet the challenge of Komendant's rigidity. In order to re-establish the curve of the cycloid at the top of the infill wall, he revised the shape of the glass lunette window. He made it narrower at the center of the cycloid where the diaphragm was widest and he made it wider at the ends of cycloid where the diaphragm was narrowest. This detail, so unlike Kahn, generated great attention in the completed building and was a superb demonstration of his artistry.

Fall of 1968, The Reflector Idea Gets Some Help

Kahn's definition of an idea was something that could be made. To take the notion of the transparent reflector into the realm of the possible required the help of someone more experienced. That someone was Richard Kelly.

Richard Kelly was thought of as the father of all lighting consultants.

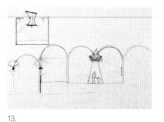

13.

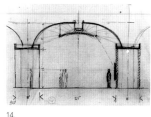

14.

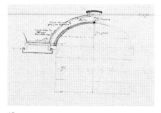

15.

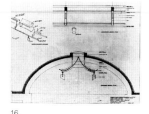

16.

He virtually founded that profession. Trained as an architect, he combined his love of the theater and the dramatic effects of stage lighting with his training in design. He recognized the characteristics of diverse kinds of light, differentiating between candlelight, the light of an overcast sky, and a light that accentuates an object or a space. Kelly was consulting on Kahn's Phillips Exeter Library Project, which was in development at the same time as the Kimbell, when, one day, Kahn showed him the large elevation drawings of the Kimbell tacked to his office wall. The scheme for the daylight reflector fascinated Kelly and he offered to help with it. At first he suggested replacing the reflector glass with plexiglas coated with a thin layer of aluminum, much the same as the original version in the model presented in November, 1967. One afternoon, at a meeting I had at his apartment in New York, he made a rough pencil sketch of the reflector shape. A curve that would "see" the scattered light of the overhead sky and reflect it onto the concrete cycloid. Soon after, we discovered that the plexiglas material would not hold this shape. In February 1969, Kelly proposed substituting aluminum reflective sheet metal, a material that was chemically polished on one surface and manufactured specifically for use in lighting fixtures. He also proposed that this material be perforated with tiny holes to give it transparency. With the right proportion of solid to void, the reflector would give the appearance of a scrim, the diaphanous curtain used for certain effects in stage productions.

Next, Kelly proposed that Isaac Goodbar, a mathematician who worked with Edison Price, a renowned manufacturer of museum light fixtures, test Kelly's reflector curve on his computer. Goodbar programmed the computer to determine the correct curve for a reflector that would read the light of the open sky as seen through a 2'-6" wide skylight and reflect that light onto the surface of a cycloid. In addition Goodbar specified that the reflected light cut off at the bottom of the cycloid and that the program also provide the coordinates of the reflector curve and foot candle readings at points along the cycloid. Goodbar's printout confirmed Kelly's intuitive sketch of the reflector curve. Armed with this information, our confidence was renewed.

Summer 1970, A Critical Impasse

Kahn's contract with the Kimbell Art Foundation required that he associate with a local architect who would advise on local conditions and regulations, produce the construction drawings, and perform the day to day field inspection. Ric Brown wrote safeguards into the contract to assure that, at all times, Kahn would maintain control of the design and he would make all design decisions. As the work progressed it became apparent that Kahn's method of working and that of the Associate Architect were not the same. Kahn worked slowly and continually made revisions to make what he sensed were improvements in the design. This caused delays in the

17.

18.

19.

20.

work. Moreover, the fee that Kahn and the Associate Architect were to share was fixed, based on a percentage of the budgeted construction cost. It is fairly well known that Kahn was not interested in making a profit from his architecture and therefore, to him, as much of the fee as possible would be spent to give him the freedom to explore design possibilities. Kahn told me that there were two kinds of architects: the "artist architect" and the "practitioner architect." Conflict arose between Kahn and the Associate Architect because of the natural tension between these approaches to the practice of architecture. Also Kahn always produced his own construction drawings because he believed they were an integral part of the design, the "how to do it."

Because of Kahn's delays and the imminent start of construction on the new Dallas/Fort Worth airport, which would impact construction costs in the area, tensions between Kahn, the Associate Architect, and the Kimbell Trustees mounted. Sometime in the summer of 1970, the Trustees instructed the Associate Architect to complete the construction drawings without benefit of Kahn's participation.

In effect, the Trustees overruled the Director and Kahn. Only after some intense behind-the-scenes negotiations with the Kimbell family, who appreciated that the building might no longer be a "Kahn" building, and after the Associate Architect wrote of his intention to terminate his contract, was the crisis resolved with an amendment

to the architectural contract, a "Clarification Agreement," which listed the duties of each architect. Kahn's control of the design was firmly established.

June, 1971, A Near Failure and Success

In January of 1970 as the reflector design was developing, Kelly added a tall fin at the top which projected up into the space below the skylight. Its purpose was two-fold: to reinforce the reflected light and to block stray light entering the galleries below. By the middle of 1971 enough of the building was constructed to allow full-size testing of reflector mock-ups under the concrete cycloid. Kelly had been concerned that, if the perforations in the aluminum reflector were too small, they could easily be clogged with airborne dust. Based on this he selected two sizes of perforation holes and hole spacing and thought that either one would provide the desired transparency, but I persisted in having both types fabricated for the site test. The Contractor isolated the test bay from ambient daylight and installed the sample reflectors. On June 21, 1971, Kahn, Kelly and I went to Fort Worth to view the installation.

Both reflectors successfully reflected daylight onto the underside of the cycloid, but only one exhibited the desired transparency. The second reflector's holes were too sparse and the reflector appeared too dense. But another problem materialized partly due to the size

21.

22.

23.

24.

25.

26.

27.

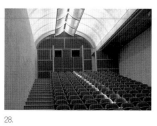
28.

of the holes. Because the cycloids were oriented north-south, at noon sun time, when the sun was at its zenith, angled sunlight would pass through the perforations and strike any south facing wall or painting. This was an intolerable situation for Brown. No art museum could function if installations on south facing walls were prohibited. At this point it appeared that the idea of transparency was doomed and Kahn was ready to abandon it in favor of a solid reflector. It was Frank Sherwood, the Associate Architect's field person, who recommended that a 2'-6" part of the reflector directly below the skylight be made of opaque aluminum. This decision effectively blocked the stray sunlight, but obscured the direct view of the sky. In the end, what saved the original idea of transparency was my realization that certain museum spaces would not exhibit works of art. The public spaces, entry hall, auditorium, banquet area, bookstore area, and library mezzanine would not require the opaque aluminum section under the skylight. Sunlight and a view of the sky were permissible in these areas and would also allow a desirable variation of light intensity. Excitedly, I immediately telephoned Ric Brown to get his reaction without first discussing it with Kahn. Both received the idea with enthusiasm and the daylighting concept was saved.

October 1972, Five Days of Celebration
Fort Worth knew how to throw a party. To celebrate the museum opening in October 1972, five days of parties were held for the construction workers, the press, national and international members of the art community, and citizens of Fort Worth. After five years of decisions, large and small, came universal acclaim for the building. Kahn stayed for one or two days of the opening festivities and then flew home in Paul Mellon's private plane. His mind was already on his other projects, most importantly the Center for British Art at Yale University of which Paul Mellor was the donor. Jules Prown, the Founding Director of the Center, told me that he had asked Ric Brown what it was like to work with Kahn. Ric had replied, "It was a lot of trouble but it was worth it."
Twenty-five years later, it's still worth it and we're still celebrating.

29.

30.

31.

32.

A Short History of the Kimbell Art Museum

The Ideal Museum

In 1931 Kay Kimbell, a wealthy entrepreneur and businessman of the food industry and his wife Velma bought their first work of art—a painting. Five years later, together with Kay's sister and her husband, they established the Kimbell Art Foundation.

Their collection expanded rapidly, albeit not in a consistently systematic fashion. In 1948, it was already on exhibition at the Fort Worth Public Library, the only location available in the city for this kind of event. Since then the question of a suitable exhibition site surfaced periodically, thus leading to the question of the development of a museum. It was only in 1964, following the death of Kay Kimbell and under the terms of his will, that the Foundation would have the necessary funds for the construction of such a museum. The city of Fort Worth allocated a plot of about 9 acres in the Will Roger Memorial Park, which already housed the Modern Art Museum of Fort Worth and the Amon Carter Museum of Western Art. However, any construction on the site had to respect a height restriction clause, so as not to obstruct the view of the city from the Amon Carter Museum.

Richard F. Brown, one of the most efficient and capable museum directors in the United States, and at that time the director of the County Museum of Los Angeles, was appointed to the administration of the Kimbell. He was to manage exhibitions and exhibits, and supervise the design of the new museum. In fact it was Brown who chose Louis I. Kahn as the design architect for the project, and cooperated closely with him for the duration of the design stage, which went on from summer 1968, and continued even when construction was already in progress. As we have mentioned elsewhere in this catalogue, the drawing up of the construction plans did not proceed without difficulty. Problems arose between Kahn and Preston M. Geren's architectural firm in Fort Worth, the company appointed to work with the Philadelphia master. Such association with a local firm was the standard practice for commissions assigned to non-resident architects. These problems, however, were soon forgotten. What does remain is the building by Louis I. Kahn, a work that Richard Brown believed could not be improved upon. The Kimbell was, in his opinion, "what every museum man has been looking for ever since museums came into existence: a floor uninterrupted by piers, columns, or windows, and perfect lighting, giving total freedom and flexibility to use the space and install art exactly the way you want", in other words: "The ideal museum is here, in Fort Worth." [L.B.]

On 27th June 1969, as he was unable to attend the ground-breaking ceremony, Louis I. Kahn wrote Mrs. Velma Kimbell a letter in which he summed up his design for the museum, and enclosed a sketch of the site layout.

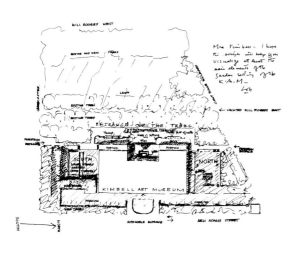

Dear Mrs Kimbell: Wednesday June 25 '69

I plan to come to see you soon to show and explain the garden ideas I have surrounding the Kimbell Art Museum. I hope you will find my work beautiful and meaningful.

The entrance of the trees is the entrance by foot which links Camp Bowie Boulevard and West Lancaster Ave. Two open porticos flank the entrance court of Terrace. In front of each portico is a reflecting pool which drops its water in a continuous sheet about 70 feet long in a basin two feet below. The sound would be gentle. The stepped entrance court passes between the porticos and their pools with a fountain, around which one sits, on axis designed to be the source of the portico pools. The west lawn gives the building perspective.

The south garden is at a level 10 feet below the garden entrance approached by gradual stepped lawns shaped to be a place to sit to watch the performance of a play music or dance the building with its arched silhouette acting as the back drop for a stage. When not so in use it will serve only as a garden where sculpture acquired from time to time would be.

The North garden though mostly utilitarian in design with ample trees to shield and balance the south and north sides of the building.

The car entrance and parking is also at the lower level running parallel to Arch Adams Street. This end too is lined with trees designed to overhang the cars as shelter. For this we must choose the right tree whose habits are respectful to the car tops.

When I see you I expect to bring a model which should say more than my little words.

By now you know that I cannot be present at the ground breaking ceremony. Unfortunately, I have emergency duties in India at the same time. In my absence I wish everything well.

I am confident that the work will progress now from now on I believe everyone believes in the building and its good purpose.

I expect to return from India by the 12th of July. I will need a few weeks to firm up the material I hope to present to you for discussion.

Sincerely yours
Louis I Kahn

The Photographic Illustration
of the Construction

A valuable photographic account by Bob Wharton
from 1969 to 1972

The Kimbell Art Museum has offered us the opportunity to exhibit and publish
a wide selection of black and white photographs which recall the history of the
Museum, from design to construction.
The events illustrated start with the signing of the construction contract on 2nd
May 1969, i.e. nearly three years after the first contact was made with the architect, and continue with the groundbreaking ceremony, the surveys to define the
location of the building on the site, excavation, structural work, formwork testing
of the architectural concrete walls, and tests performed on the shells of the
vaults, the architect's visits on the site, ending with the final inspection and the
handing over of the building on 3rd August 1972. Many of these pictures are
being exhibited and published for the first time. They were taken by Bob Wharton, the official photographer of the Kimbell Art Museum, who covered the activities of the Museum from the very beginning. The late Bob Wharton is responsible for the meticulous documentation of The Kimbell Art Museum in its early
years. His own interest in the individuals involved and fascination with the process taking place led him far beyond routine photographic recording of events
and actual construction. He is responsible as well for the photographs illustrating the first decade of the museum's existence.
Cassandra Weyandt has skillfully printed Bob Wharton's original negatives for
the catalogue.
[L.B.-P.C.L.]

1.

1. 2. 3. 4.
Louis I. Kahn at the formal meeting to sign
the construction contract for the Kimbell
Art Museum, Fort Worth, May 2, 1969
5. 6. 7.
Louis I. Kahn presenting the project for the
Kimbell Art Museum, using model made in
Fort Worth to assist with cost estimates and
his own model, during the press
conference after the construction contract
was signed, Fort Worth, May 2, 1969

5. 6. 7.

2. 3. 4.

8.9.

8. 9. 10.
More pictures of Louis I. Kahn during the
presentation of the project, Fort Worth,
2 May 1969

10.

11.
Aerial view of the site of the museum with downtown Forth Worth in the background, January 1969
12. 13. 14
Aerial views of the site during construction and at completion of work, January 1971, February 1971 and June 1972

12.

13.

14.

15.

16.

17.

18.

19.

20.

19. 20.
Test pouring of concrete walls with
special formwork to obtain raised joints,
October 30, 1969
21.
The auditorium during the construction
of the walls and the installation
of ventilation ducts, November 1970
22.
Reinforcing bars for the main staircase,
May 15, 1970.

22.

21.

24.

25.

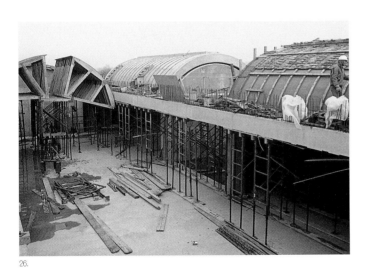

26.

27.

28. 29. 30. 31. 32.
Casting of the cycloid vault, installation of
the lead roof lining, January and June 1971

28.

29.30.31.

32.

33.
Installation of travertine panels onto
non-bearing walls, September 1971
34.
Completion of the courtyard facing the
main entrance, May 1972

34.

35.
Louis I. Kahn, Richard Brown, Marshall D.
Meyers and others at the final inspection,
August 3, 1972
36.
Louis I. Kahn in the auditorium,
August 3, 1972

35.

36.

37. 38.

39.

40.

The Design Stage
From the beginning of 1967 to the end of 1968

Two years of design drawings before completion
of the final site plan

The First Design or "Square-Plan"

Spring 1967 Plans

Richard Brown became director of the Kimbell Art Museum in February 1966, and met Kahn for the first time in his Philadelphia architecture office in April of that same year. On 5th October a contract was signed between Louis I. Kahn and the Kimbell Art Foundation whereby a preliminary project was to be delivered within six months, the building completed by 1st September 1969, and fully installed by 1st March of the following year.

Louis I. Kahn only kept to the first deadline, presenting a model to a scale of 1:1200 which indicated how the building would be positioned on the lot assigned by the City of Fort Worth in the Will Rogers Memorial Park. This early project was referred to as the "Square-Plan." It showed a large, wide structure which occupied a considerable part of the building area, with a partially usable basement floor, and a main level composed of long parallel trapezoidal vaulted units. If, on the one hand, the solution presented was rather empirical with regard to space and surface area, on the other, it nevertheless displayed the basic characteristics of the research which led the architect to his final design. The question of natural light filtering in from the roof and courtyards was addressed, and there is clear evidence of the idea of blending the different areas by the repetition of simple, functional units. That first stage already included the natural light reflectors, and would require long and in-depth studies into the correct refraction and the appropriate materials needed to obtain this.

One of Kahn's perspective drawings is particularly noteworthy and anticipatory: it is reproduced on the next page and bears the number 730.194 from the well-known Garland catalogue in which all of Louis I. Kahn's drawings are featured. With a few charcoal strokes Kahn shows us the vaults and the continuing spaces beyond the loadbearing structures, the daylight reflectors, as well as the proportions between the different components.

Patricia Cummings Loud describes the plan of the first preliminary project for the Kimbell Art Museum on page 111 of her book, titled *The Art Museums of Louis Kahn*: "In the plan it can be seen that the square shape of the whole is due to the arcade. Essentially there are two long, rectangular parts, three vaulted units on the west and six on the east, surrounded by the arcade and porches. The two sections are included in the main west-east axis. The lower-floor plan indicates little development other than parking and an automobile drive-through." [L.B.]

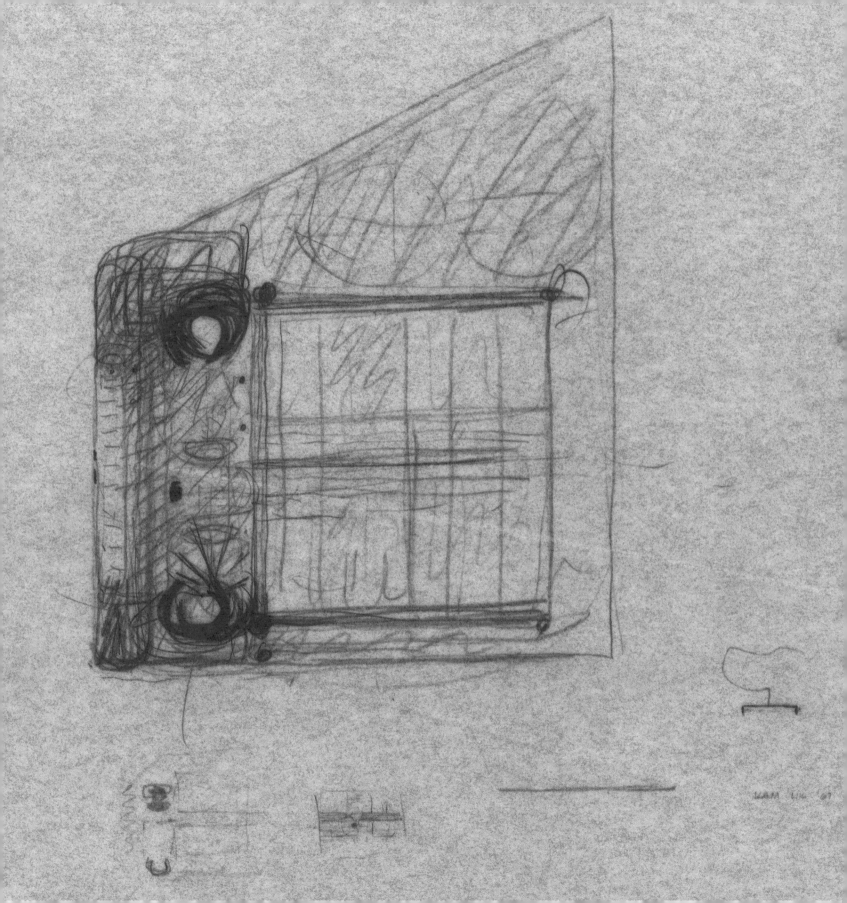

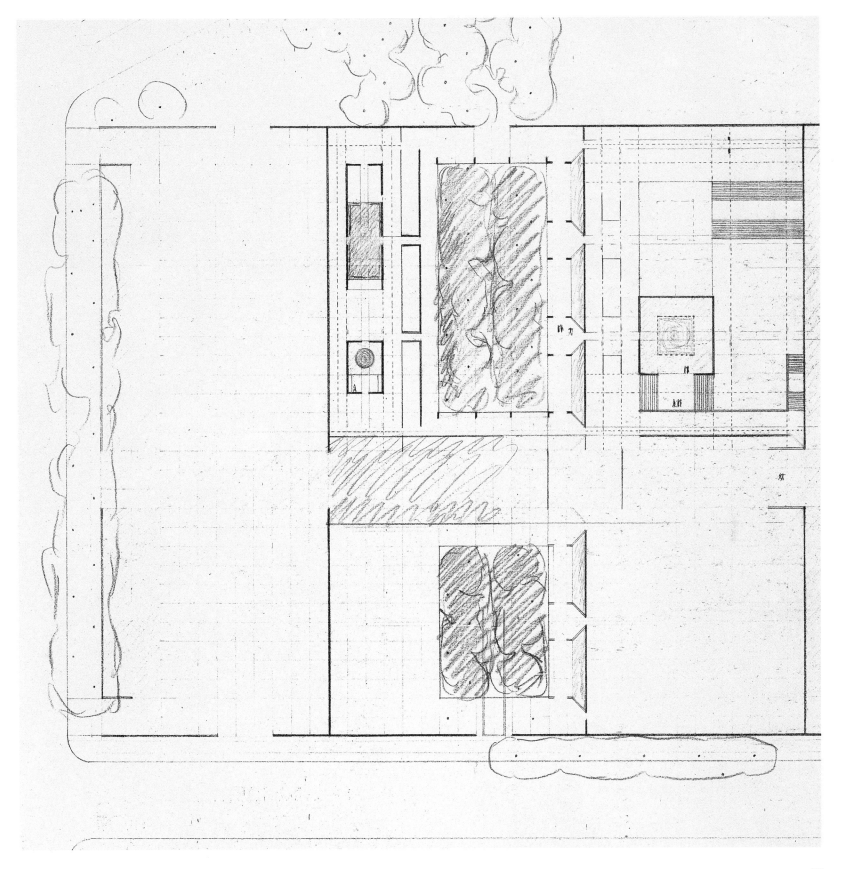

The Design Stage

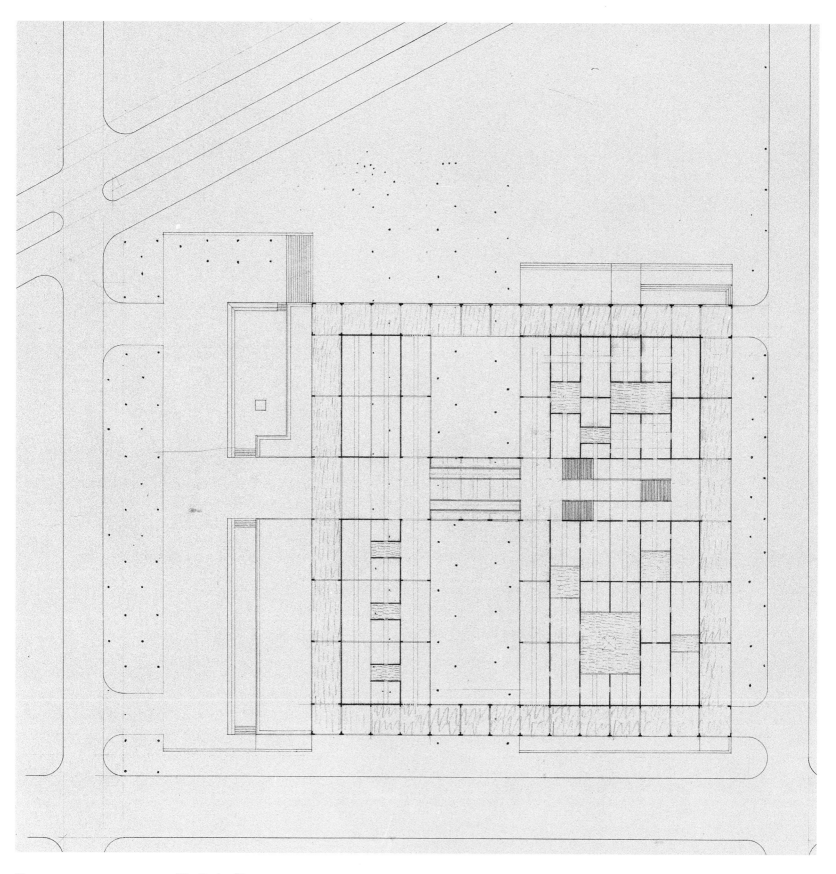

previous page
Lower level plan (scale 1:1200), spring 1967

Upper level plan (scale 1:900), spring 1967

The Second Design or "H-Plan"

Plans from July to November 1967

At the end of the summer Louis I. Kahn asked Marshall D. Meyers, with whom he had already worked from 1957 to 1965, to help him deliver the Kimbell Art Museum Project that had been lying on his desk since the first broad—albeit essential—drawings of March 1967.

When Meyers returned to Kahn's office in August 1967, developments in the project were progressing slowly with modifications to the first proposal. However, in September, a whole series of prospective drawings, elevations and schemes—the "H-Plan"—was completed.

Although the planimetric outcome did not differ in any substantial way from the first version, the plans gave a clearer notion of the actual structure of the building. Moreover, the trapezoidal roof structure was substituted by a vaulted one, which already approached the cycloid shape Marshall D. Meyers suggested the following month of December.

Patricia Cummings Loud described this second version on page 113 of the above-mentioned book as follows: "The new plan no longer includes connecting north and south arcades and east portico; thus the garden courtyards with trees, formerly internal, open directly onto surrounding lawns. [...] The west pavilion consists of two longitudinal vaults plus a third as a porch, while the east consists of seven. The vaulted shape, now more spreading and Mediterranean, has a thin reflector, projected to be made of glass, beneath the skylight. These vaults are spaced alternately with flat channels, which in this second design have become Kahn's service spaces for ducts and conduits."

It is on the basis of this project that August Komendant and Richard Kelly started work on the structural engineering and lighting aspects, respectively.

In November a new development took place, and, after a series of functional tests and budget estimates, the second project was presented once again in its modified version in July of the following year.

Basically the various permutations of the second project resulted in the reduction of the surface area and the courtyards, as well as in an improved utilization of the lower floor. All this was achieved without changes to the basic layout of the project. [L.B.]

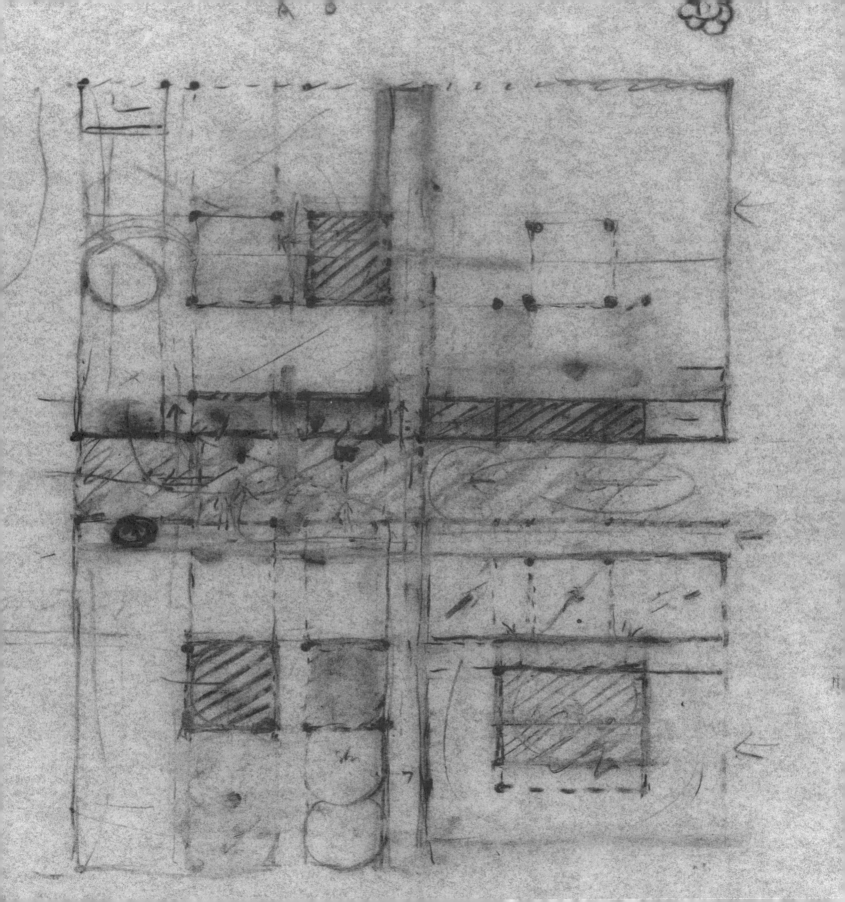

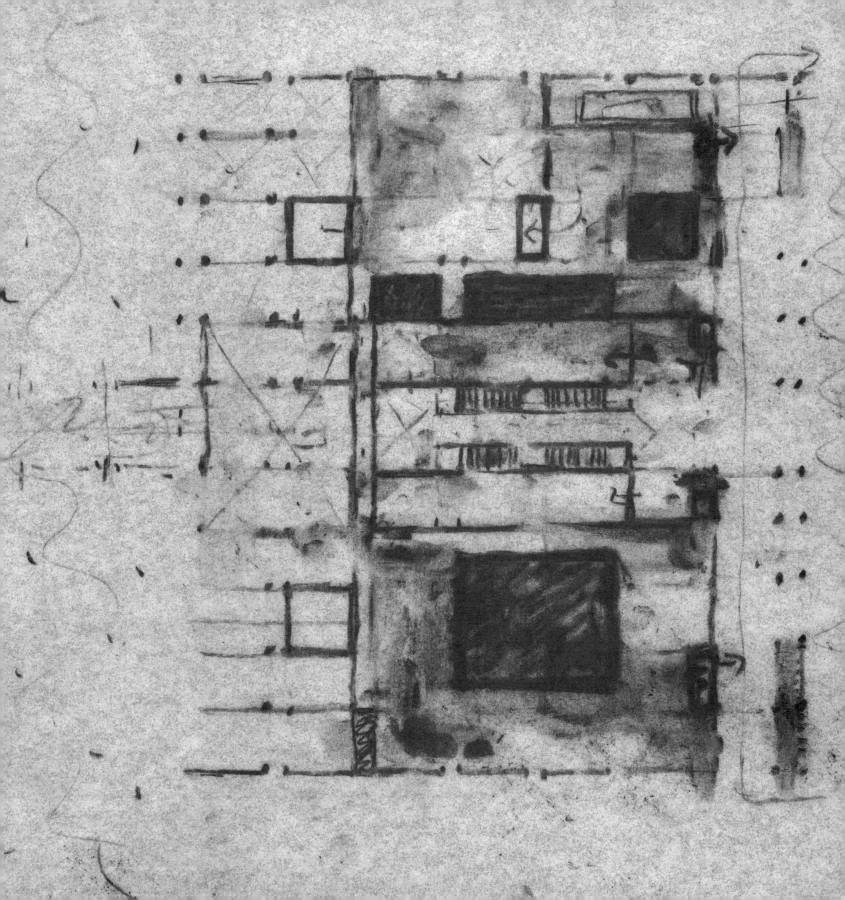

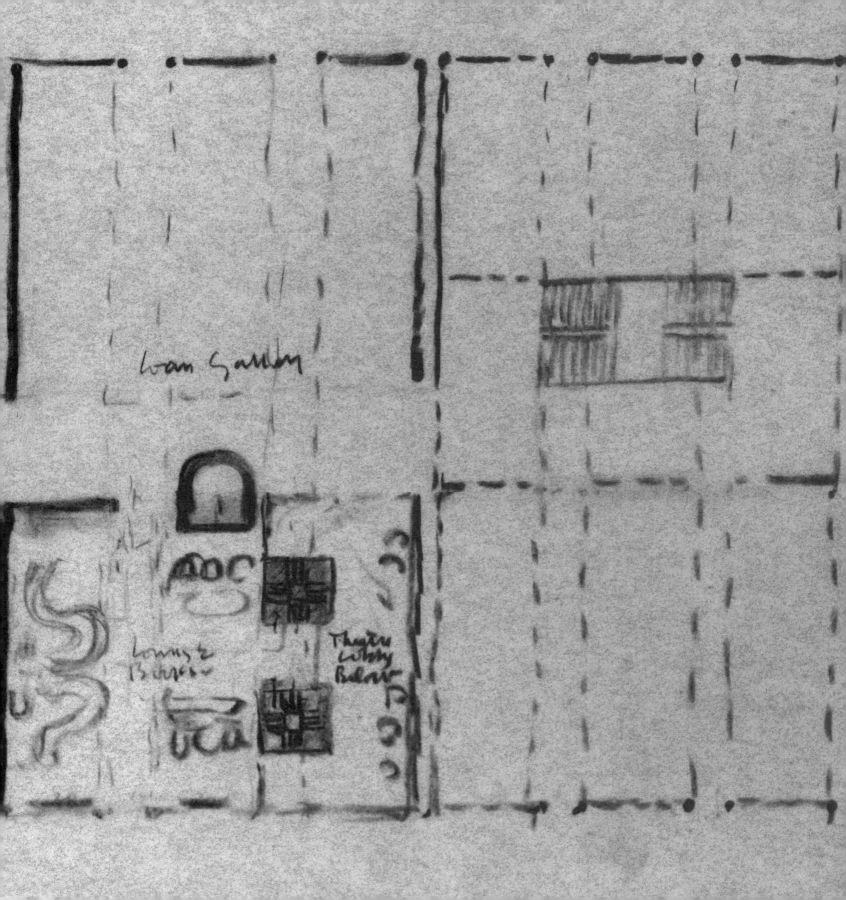

60'

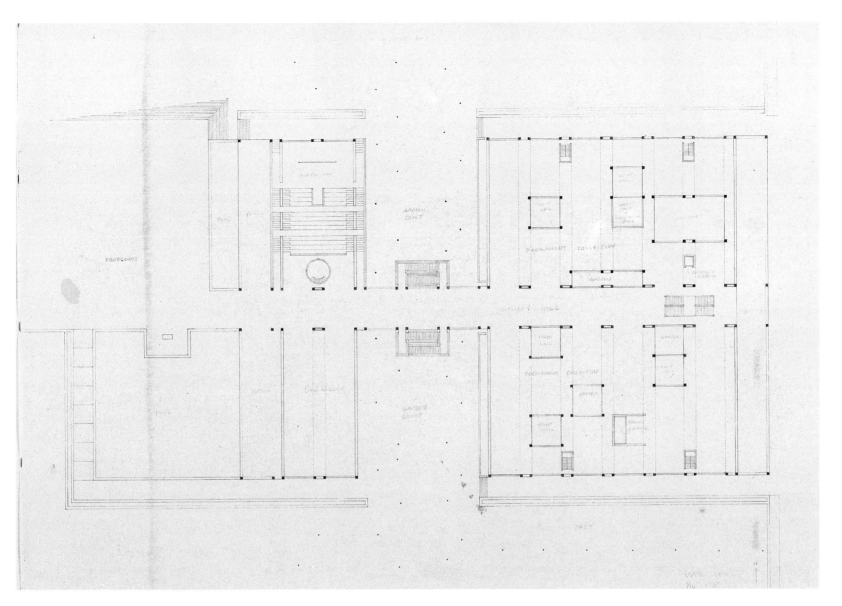

First version of the H-Plan (scale 1:900),
upper level, November-December 1967

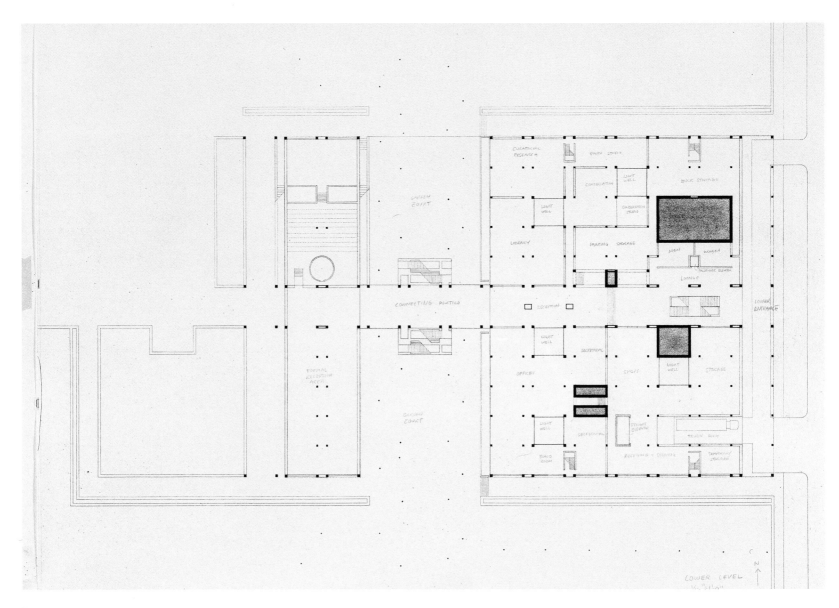

First version of the H-Plan (scale 1:900),
lower level plan November-December 1967

The Design Stage

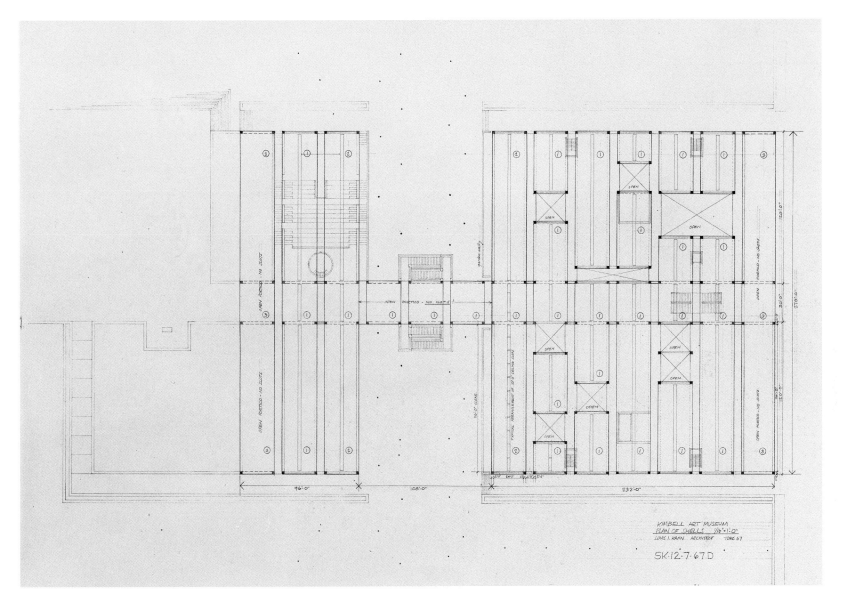

First version of the H-Plan (scale 1:900),
plan of shells, December 1967

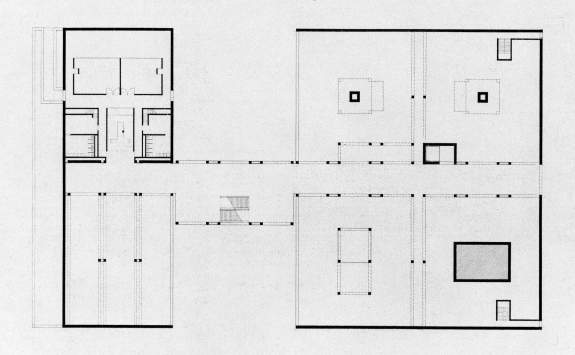

Second version of the H-Plan, (scale 1:900),
lower level, July 1968

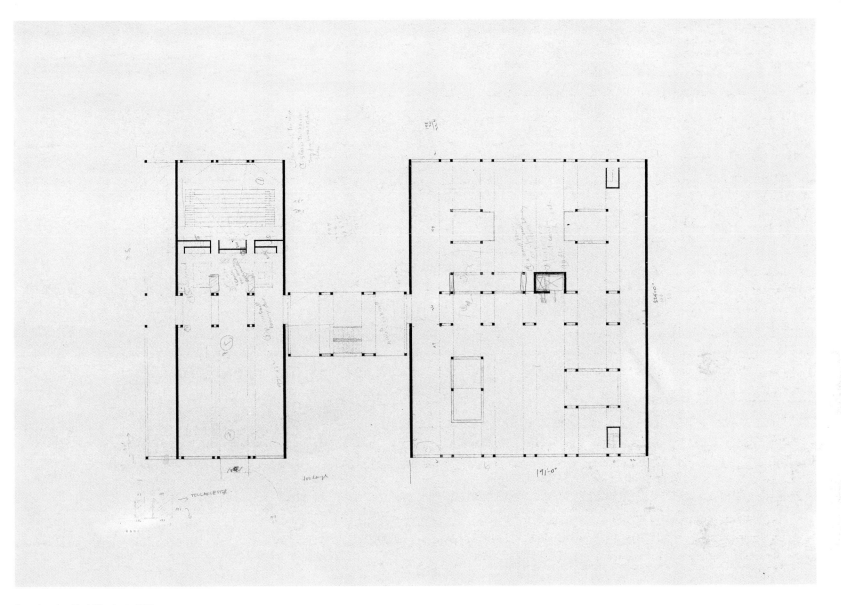

Second version of the H-Plan (scale 1:900),
upper leve, July 1968

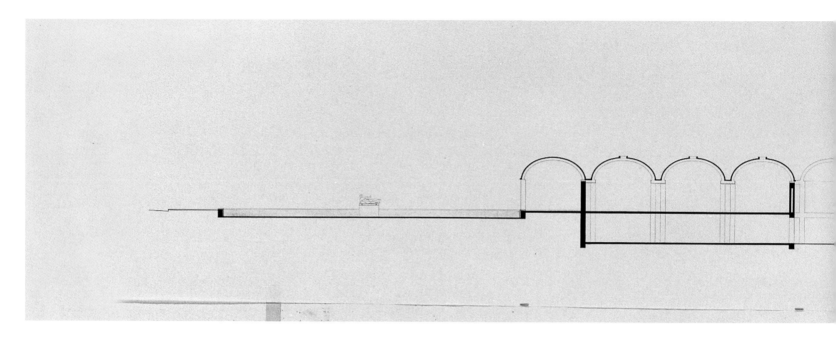

Second version of the H-Plan (scale 1:450),
cross section, July 1968

The Design Stage

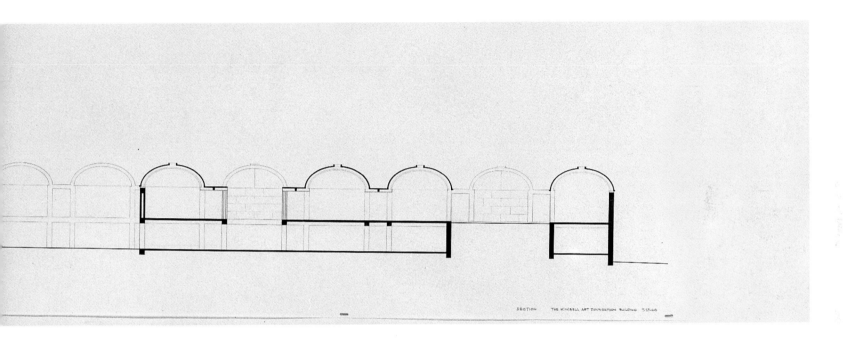

SECTION   THE KIMBELL ART FOUNDATION BUILDING 7-17-68

The Third Design or "C-Plan"

Plans from September to November 1968

The project took a decisive turn in August 1968 and, before the end of September, a new series of plans was sent out to Fort Worth. These plans showed a C-shaped building, which was the final form the museum would take. The project followed an axial scheme comprising one smaller central element flanked by two larger ones, forming a front court that clearly leads into the museum.
The porches are now defined, and so is the structure: the vaults are sustained solely by columns, to offer plenty of useable space, while the unbroken walls are located on the perimeter or around the courtyards. The large pool in front of the entrance was to be deleted from the final version of the project.

On page 124 of her book Patricia Cummings Loud thus described the main characteristics of this third version of the preliminary project: "The most obvious changes in the third design are seen in the building's shape and its relationship to the oddly configured trapezoidal site. Now the building consists of a central unit with two north and south wings projecting to either side and forming a forecourt. [...] The complete museum with its recessed forecourt is located on the site's east end, behind the rows of trees, and the perimeter of the site there is enriched with plantings."
During the following months, this third version of the preliminary project gave rise to the final version which would eventually be realized. [L.B.]

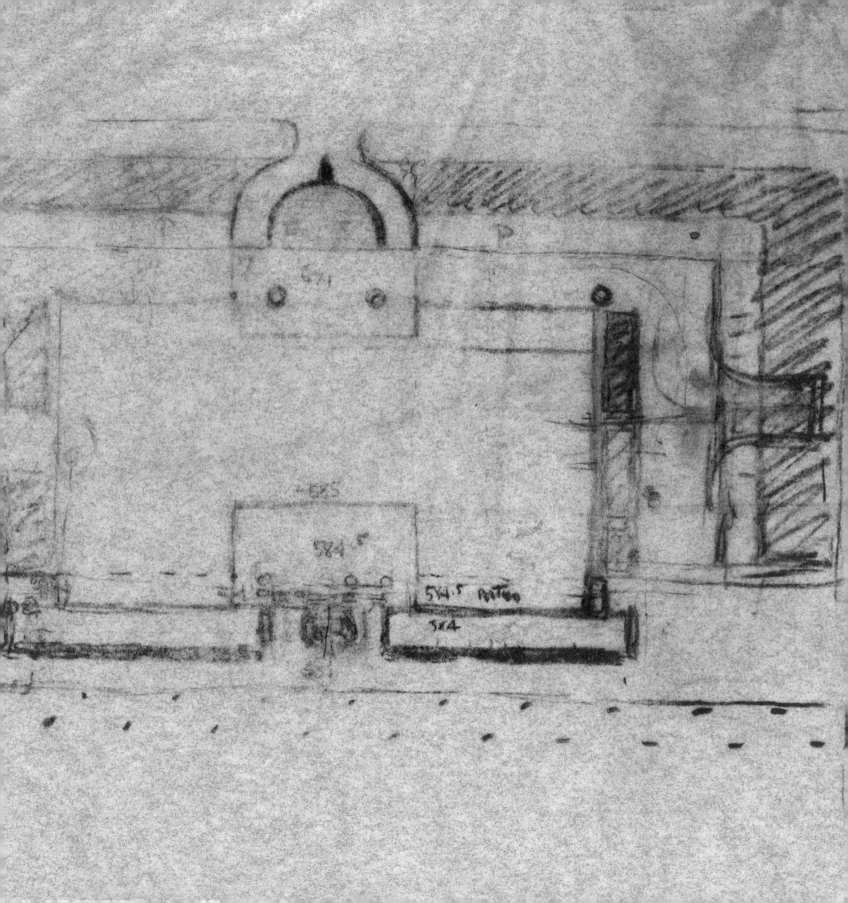

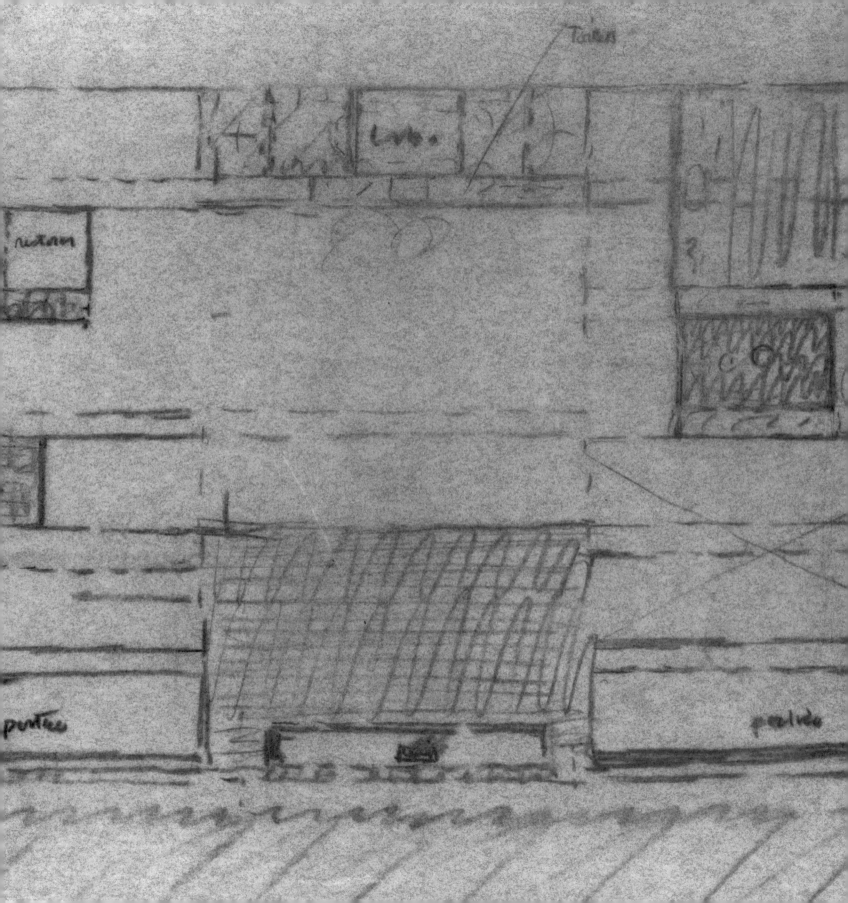

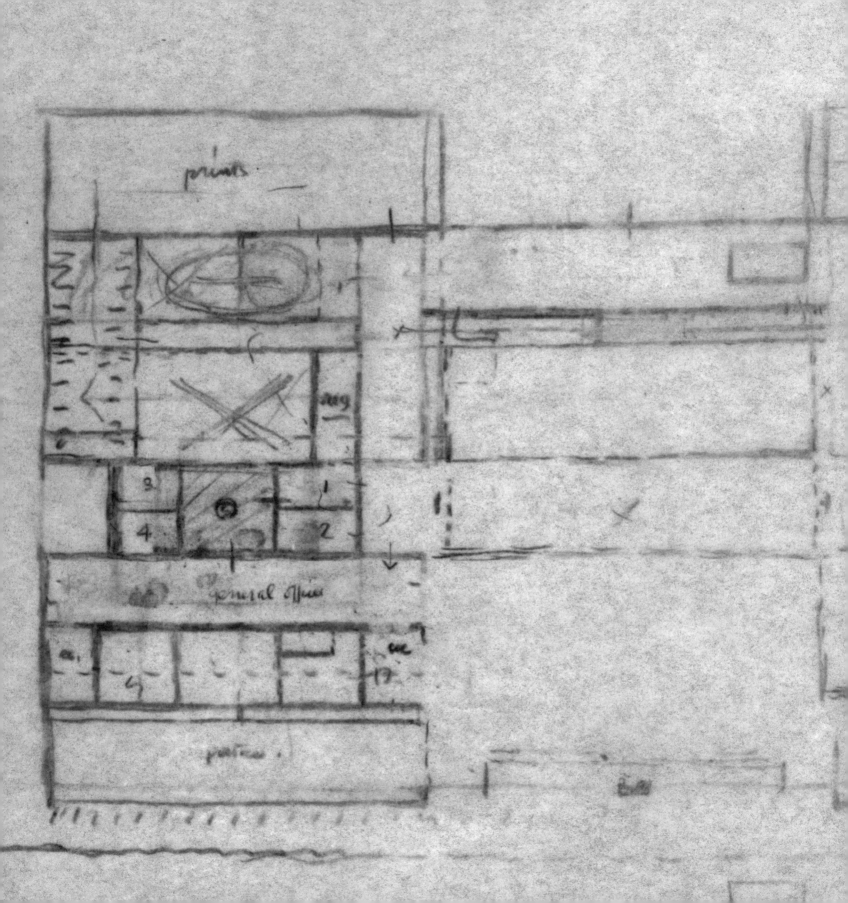

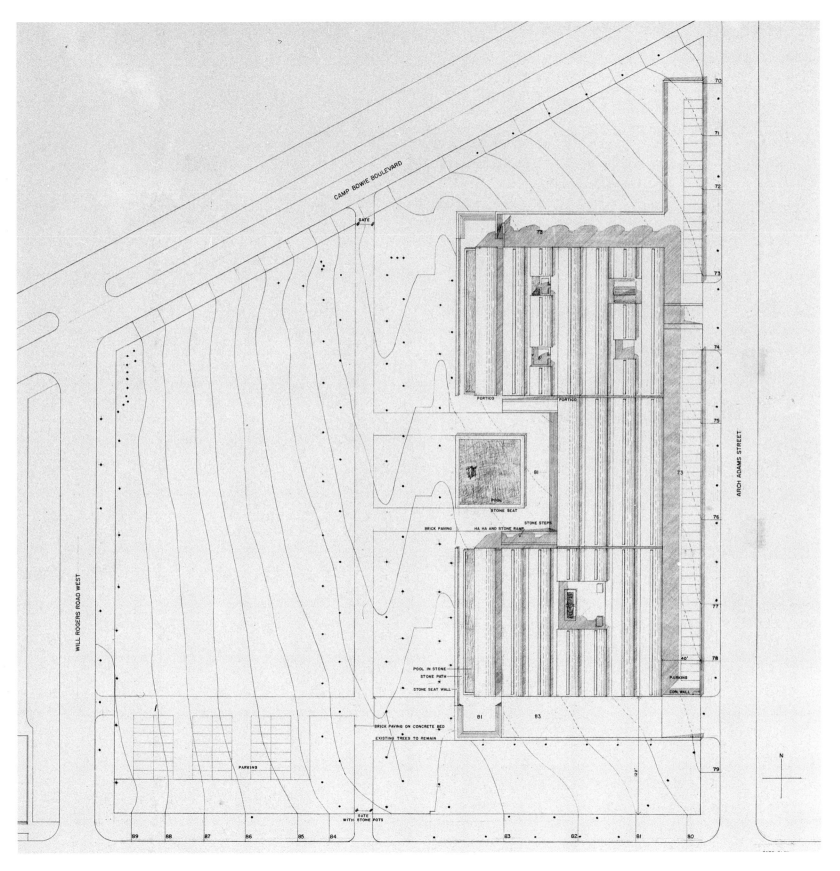

CAMP BOWIE BOULEVARD

GATE

70

71

72

73

PORTICO PORTICO

74

75

ARCH ADAMS STREET

81

POOL

STONE SEAT

73

76

BRICK PAVING

HA HA AND STONE RAMP

STONE STEPS

WILL ROGERS ROAD WEST

77

POOL IN STONE

STONE PATH

STONE SEAT WALL

40'

78

PARKING

CON. WALL

81

83

BRICK PAVING ON CONCRETE BED

EXISTING TREES TO REMAIN

79

122'

N

PARKING

GATE
WITH STONE POTS

89 88 87 86 85 84

83 82 81 80

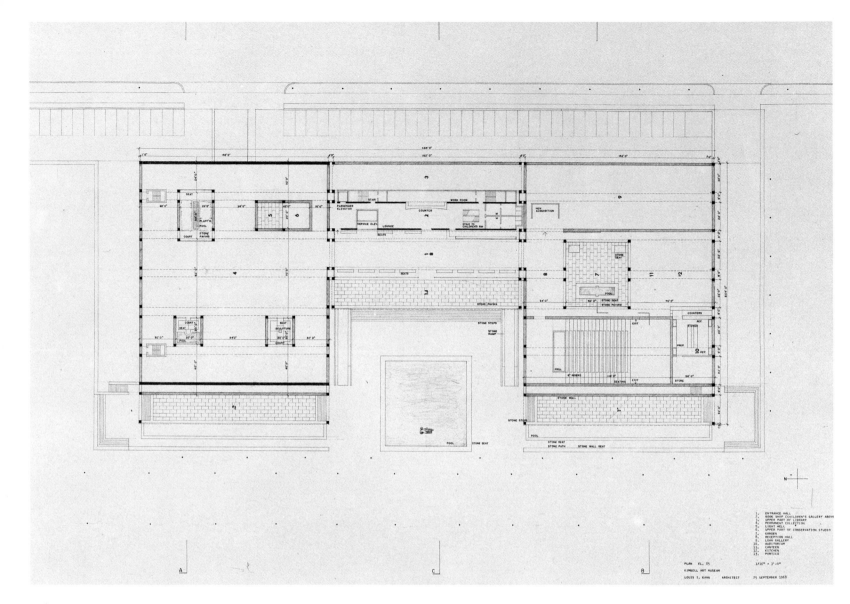

previous page
Site plan (scale 1:1200) 25 September 1968

First version of C-Plan, upper level plan
(scale 1:900), September 1968

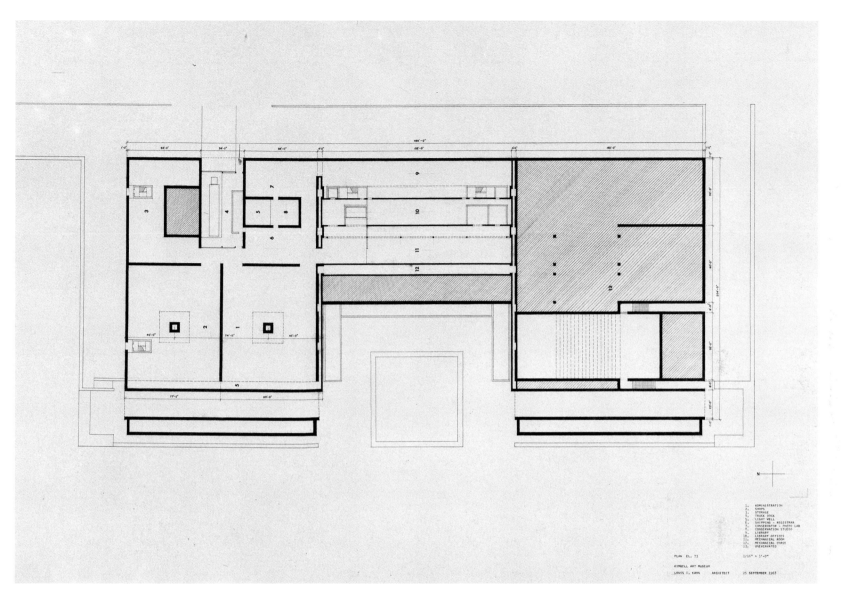

PLAN EL. 73   1/16" = 1'-0"

KIMBELL ART MUSEUM

LOUIS I. KAHN   ARCHITECT   25 SEPTEMBER 1968

First version of C-Plan, lower level plan,
(scale 1:900), September 1968

The Design Stage   93

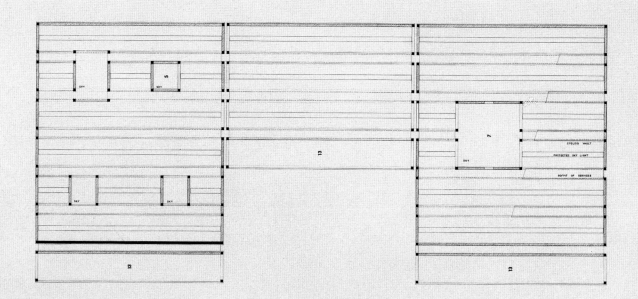

First version of C-Plan, reflected ceiling
plan (scale 1:900), September 1968

The Design Stage

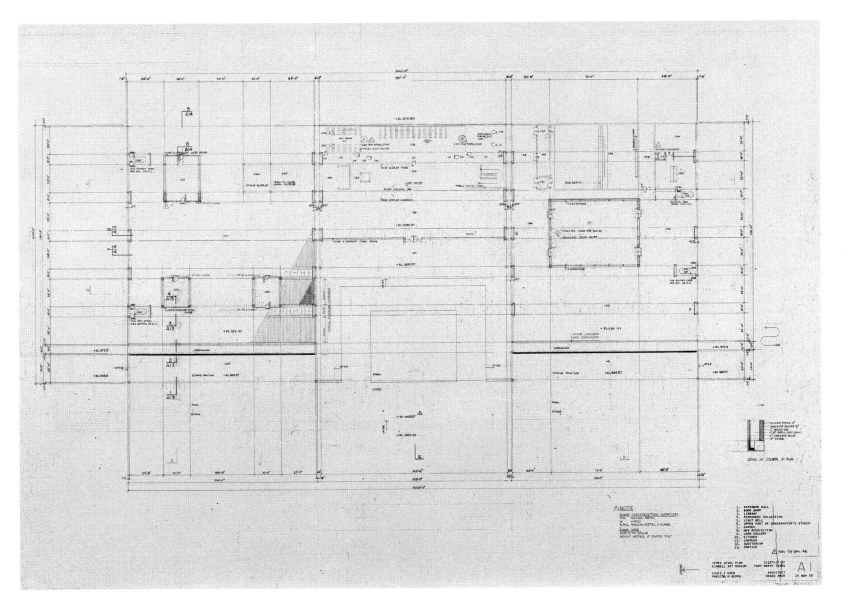

Second version of C-Plan, upper level plan
(scale 1:900), November 1968

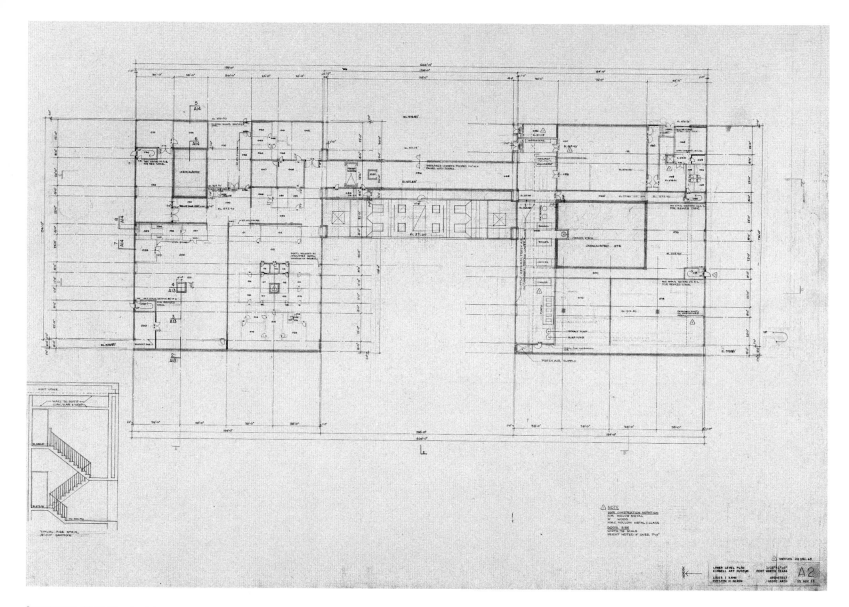

Second version of C-Plan lower level plan
(scale 1:900), November 1968

Second version of C-Plan, cross section,
the entrance court (scale 1:450),
November 1968

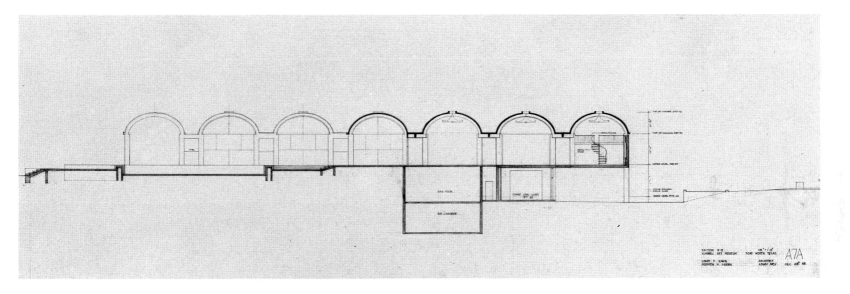

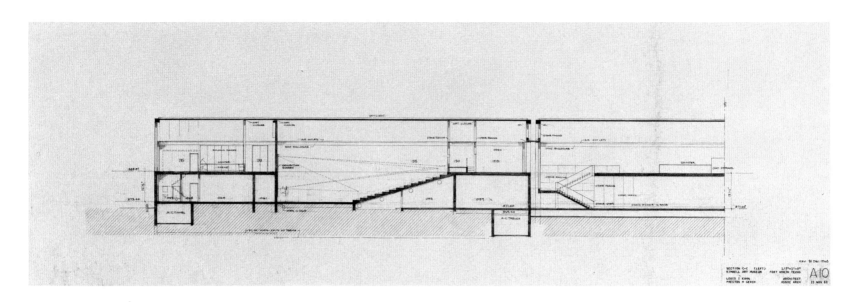

Second version of C-Plan, longitudinal
section, north side (scale 1:450),
November 1968

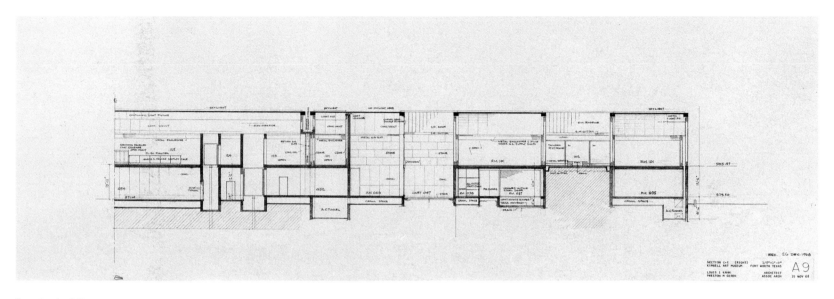

Second version C-Plan, longitudinal
section south side , (scale 1:450),
November 1968

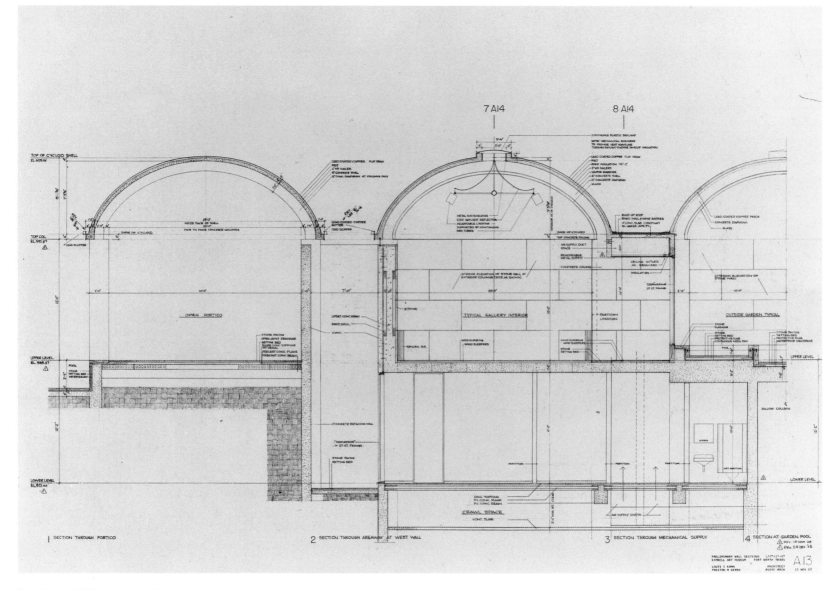

Second version of C-Plan, preliminary wall
section (scale 1:110), November 1968

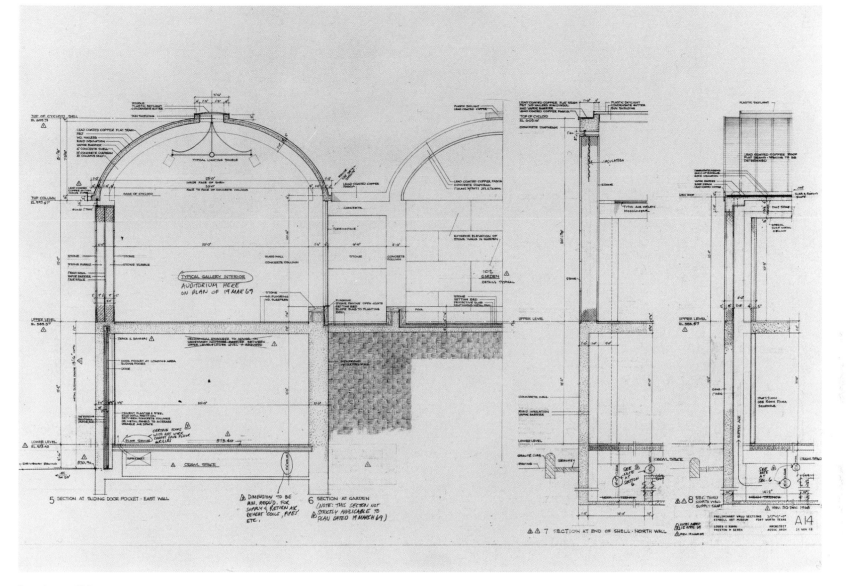

Second version of C-Plan, preliminary wall
section (scale 1:110), November 1968

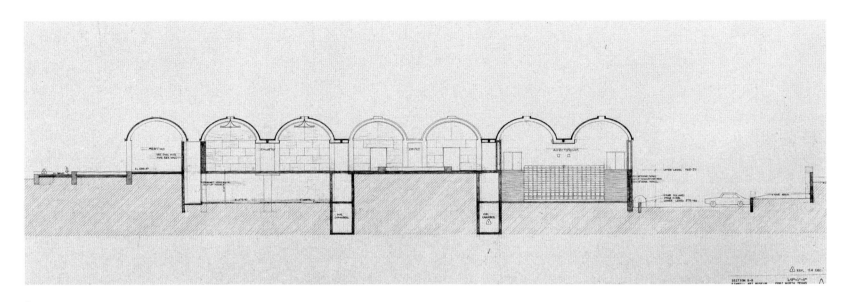

Cross section, auditorium
(scale 1:450), November 1968

The Structure

An Analysis of the Structure

Aurelio Muttoni

[1] August E. Komendant, *18 Years with Architect Louis I. Kahn*, Aloray Publisher Englewood N.J., 1975.

[2] Patricia Cummings Loud, The *Art Museums of Louis I. Kahn*, Duke University Press, Durham and London, 1989, pp. 108-110.

[3] Marshall D. Meyers, *Making the Kimbell, A Brief Memoir*.

[4] Fred Angerer, *Bauen mit Tragenden Flächen*, Verlag Georg D.W.Callwey, München 1960.

[5] Franz Dischinger, *Ulrich Finsterwalder, Eisenbetonschalendächer, System Zeiss-Dywidag, Der Bauingenieur*, Heft 44-46, 1928.

[6] August E. Komendant, *Practical Structural Analysis for Architectural Engineering*, Prentice-Hall, N.J., 1987.

Almost all of the Kimbell Art Museum's structural components are easily identifiable. Not only do the shapes of the structure fully respect the requirements of statics, but they also become fundamental elements from the architectural point of view. In this building, cooperation with the structural engineer proved most important. As with other projects, which include the Medical Research Laboratory in Philadelphia, the First Unitarian Church in Rochester, the Salk Institute in La Jolla and the Olivetti-Underwood Factory Building in Harrisburg, Kahn could avail himself of Dr. August Komendant's[1] cooperation for the Kimbell Museum project.

The most interesting structural element is certainly the roof, which is visible from the exhibit rooms, and is composed of a series of prestressed reinforced concrete shells, each supported by four columns. Although the roof spans 102 feet (31.059 m) lengthwise and 22 feet (6.710 m) crosswise, the unique structural shape has kept the thickness of the shells to a mere 4 inches (102 mm).

The choice of roof was not based on structural requirements. Since his very first drawings, Kahn had imagined a series of vaulted galleries with an aperture at the top, so as to admit daylight. His sketches[2] show that he considered different shapes (e.g. cylindrical, trapezoidal and flat), always dwelling on the effect of light filtering through the skylight, and being reflected onto the intrados.

As Marshall Meyers points out in his contribution to this catalogue[3], the choice of structure, and above all its shape, was influenced by Fred Angerer's book on surface structures in architecture[4]. Meyers, who at that time was working for Kahn on the Kimbell Museum project, was probably intrigued by the examples of thin reinforced concrete shells described by Angerer, and especially by the idea of covering a considerable span using a structure that was open at the top (Figures 1 and 2). Different shapes of shells were compared in Angerer's book, such as semi-circle, ellipse, cycloid and sector of a circle (Figure 3). Meyers and Kahn opted for the cycloid shape, which seemed better suited to their requirements. The cycloid is a curve generated by a point on the circumference of a circle which rolls, without slipping, on a straight line. This shape is not very different from that of the ellipse (Figure 4). However, from a mathematical point of view, it is cyclical, exactly like the roof elements of the Kimbell Museum. Another characteristic of the cycloid is the ratio between its width and height, which must be π.

This type of structure was developed by Franz Dischinger who patented[5] it in 1923. Dischinger discovered, in particular, that barrel shells with a vertical tangent near the longitudinal edge area, as found in both elliptical and cycloidal shapes, do not require a thrust corresponding to these edges, since the whole load rests on both ends. Their behavior is thus completely different from that of a vault, and resembles more that of a beam. In those years analytical solutions were being developed mainly in Germany to describe such behavior on the basis of the mem-

[7] Stefan Polónyi, *Wissenschaftsvertändnis, Tragkonstruktion, Architektur,* Auszug aus dem Vortrag *Revision des Wissenschaftsverständnisses* anlässlich der Verleihung der Ehrendoktorwürde der Gesamthochschule, Kassel, 1987.

brane theory and the general theory of shells. The former provides extremely simple solutions compared to the very complex computations required by the latter. However, conditions at the edges must be taken into account by the addition of stringers along the longitudinal edges and diaphragms at both ends.

Komendant had studied in Germany, and was familiar with this kind of research. In fact, he dedicated more than ten pages of his last publication[6] to an analysis of this problem. The Kimbell Art Museum roofing scheme demonstrates his concern for the respect of static conditions so as to allow a simple analytical approach. The resulting structure is composed of three elements: a uniformly thin shell whose geometrical shape can be described by a simple mathematical formula, stringers that are structurally distinct from the shell (Figure 5), and arch-shaped end diaphragms (Figure 6).

The structure may be described as a combination of tensile and compressional stressed areas (Figure 7). The load at the crown is absorbed by a series of transversal arches due to the inclusion of small reinforced concrete struts placed across the skylights. The thrust of these transversal arches is gradually transmitted to another series of arches that span lengthwise. The stress of the longitudinal arches is counteracted at both ends by ties made up of post-tensioning tendons while its tangential component is transmitted to the end diaphragms as shear force. The forces are conveyed to the top of the columns through the two arch-

shaped diaphragms. On the longitudinal edges, where the longitudinal arches rest on the lower ties, shear forces are also present, and are transmitted to the stringers, which are stressed by pure tension.

The functioning, with carrying action along its length as well as crosswise, is thus very different from that of an ordinary vault. The roof of the Kimbell Museum has often been compared with those realized by Le Corbusier in the fifties and sixties. From the structural point of view, stress in the vaults by Le Corbusier is absorbed by arches that unload the entire vertical component of the thrust onto walls or longitudinal beams, and the horizontal component onto ties or contiguous vaults (Figures 8, 9 and 10). It is worth noting that the different functions depend primarily upon the shape: a thin cycloid shell for the Kimbell and a circular section vault, very close to the load link polygon, for the Jaoul and Sarabhai houses by Le Corbusier.

The presence of skylights in the Kimbell Museum may incorrectly lead one to think of a series of elements that are structurally separated by the apertures. In this case we would have simple longitudinal beams whose upper part would act transversally like a cantilever. This, however, would require much greater thickness of the shell, and the deformation of the edge along the skylights would pose a problem.

In addition to the shell, the stringers and the end diaphragms have a shape that is also perfectly compatible with their structural function. In the first phase of the project, the stringers were designed different-

ly (Figure 11). Kahn not only respected the requirements of plant engineering, but also intended to add actual marginal beams to support the vaults vertically. After Komendant had explained that the stringers did not have that kind of loadbearing function, but were in fact suspended from the shell and subjected to pure tension, the design was changed to its present form (1, p. 124).

Even the arch-shaped end diaphragm was slightly modified. Introduced by Komendant to allow the transmission of shear force to the supports, it was, as described by Marshall Meyers, only 2 feet (0.610 m) wide, and had a constant thickness of 1 foot (0.305 m). At first the functioning of this element was probably not fully understood, not even by Komendant. Despite the arch shape, and although the forces acting on the columns are in a vertical direction, the functioning is that of a beam; highly stressed in the central part by a strong tensile force, and having to function as a tie. After the initial calculations necessary to establish cost estimates, Komendant in fact doubled the height at the top and reinforced the element with a transversal post-tensioning tendon that was later to be replaced by a stronger reinforcement (Figure 12). Kahn and Meyers were not enthusiastic about this shape. There were various alternative designs presented which consisted of a variable or increased section diaphragm along the entire length (Figure 13), with a glass window lunette that separated the structural element from the underlying wall, and maintained a constant width of 4 inches as in the preliminary project. In the end Kahn accepted Komendant's suggestion to express the structural action with a variable height shape, but he then modified the glass lunette by widening it where the diaphragm was thinnest, and maintaining a minimum width where the diaphragm was thickest.

The roof of the Kimbell Museum, like the other parts of its structure, is an example of "constructive honesty" where form and structural function are closely associated. Considering it is not always easy to understand structural functioning, both questions posed by Polónyi[7] remain unanswered: "For whom must the loadbearing structure be decipherable, and to what level of detail must it permit decipherment?"

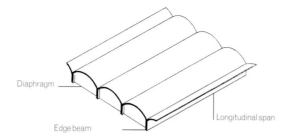

Diaphragm

Edge beam

Longitudinal span

1.

2.

3.

Ellipse
Cycloid
Catenary

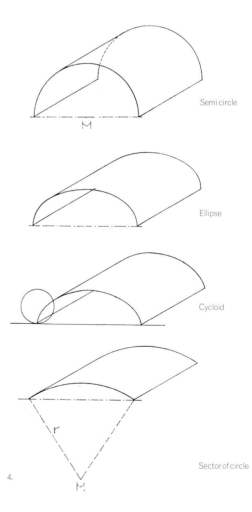

Semi circle

Ellipse

Cycloid

Sector of circle

4.

An Analysis of the Structure

1.
Series of thin shells described by Angerer[4]
2.
An example of shell with a skylight at the top provided by Angerer[4]
3.
A comparison between cycloid, ellipse and catenary
4.
A comparison of the different geometrical shapes referred to by Marshall Meyers[3]
5.
Transversal section of cycloid-shaped shells
6.
Arch-shaped end diaphragms

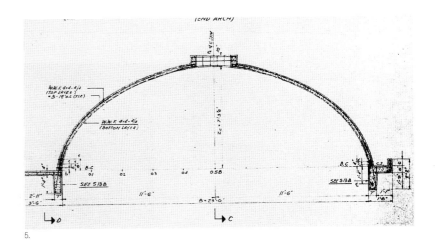

5.

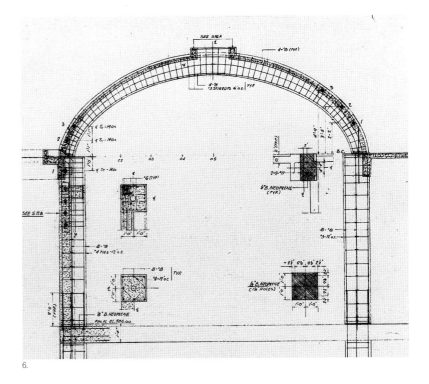

6.

An Analysis of the Structure

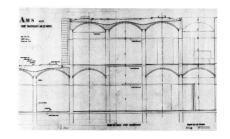

8.9.

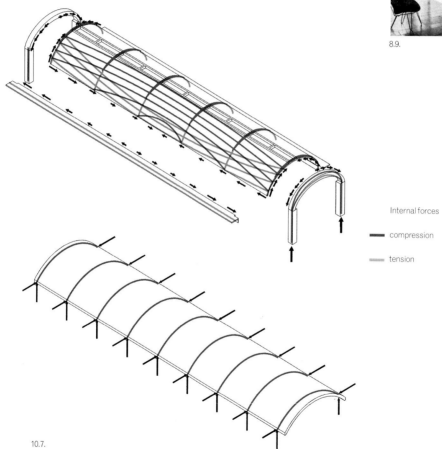

Internal forces

━━ compression

━━ tension

10.7.

An Analysis of the Structure

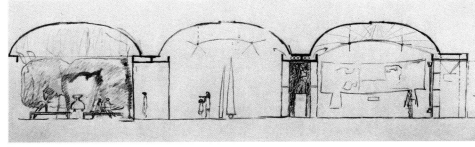

11.

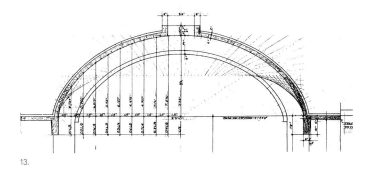

13.

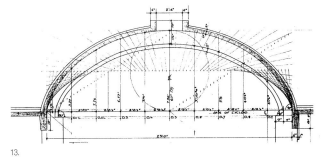

13.

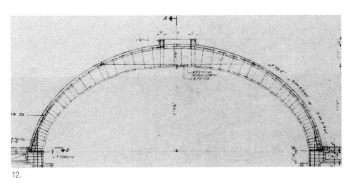

12.

Drawing Up the Construction Plans

From spring 1969 to summer 1970. From Louis Kahn's Design Sketches to Preston M. Geren's Construction Drawings

On the basis of Louis I. Kahn's plans, Preston M. Geren's architectural office produced a series of forty construction drawings which comprised all information pertaining to the building, from the actual structural work to walls and window frames, including fixtures, and wall and floor coverings, ceilings, carpentry and metal work. Twelve of the most significant of these plans, all dated June 1970, are reproduced here.

The Final Design

The final Design and drawing up of the construction plans were characterized by a series of delays and misunderstandings between the offices of both architects. It had been agreed that the construction plans, management and on site inspections would be taken care of by Preston M. Geren and Associates in Fort Worth. This is common practice, due in part to the considerable distances involved, as well as to problems regarding the different legislations pertaining to building regulations in different states, and to the question of project approval by local authorities. Moreover, one should not forget that at that time Louis I. Kahn was involved in several other projects, including the Management Institute at Ahmedabad in India and the Parliament building in Dacca, the new capital of Bangladesh.

As a result, when it came to progressing from design to construction, several problems arose. On the one hand, Preston M. Geren considered the design stage should end with the drawing up of the construction plans. On the other hand, Louis I. Kahn tended to believe that both the design and construction drawings had to develop in a continuous and complementary way. The disagreement was profound, and caused a considerable amount of resentment between both parties. This in turn created friction and delays, and Geren felt compelled to draw the client's attention to the fact that his office was forced into irregular work patterns in order to complete the construction plans on time. The contract, however, clearly defined both the deadlines to be kept by Kahn, and his responsibilities regarding the design.

The construction work, which should have commenced one year after the signing of the contract, on 5th October 1966, could only officially begin on 30th July 1969. The search for the perfect solution took Kahn longer than expected, and continued well into the construction phase. [L.B.]

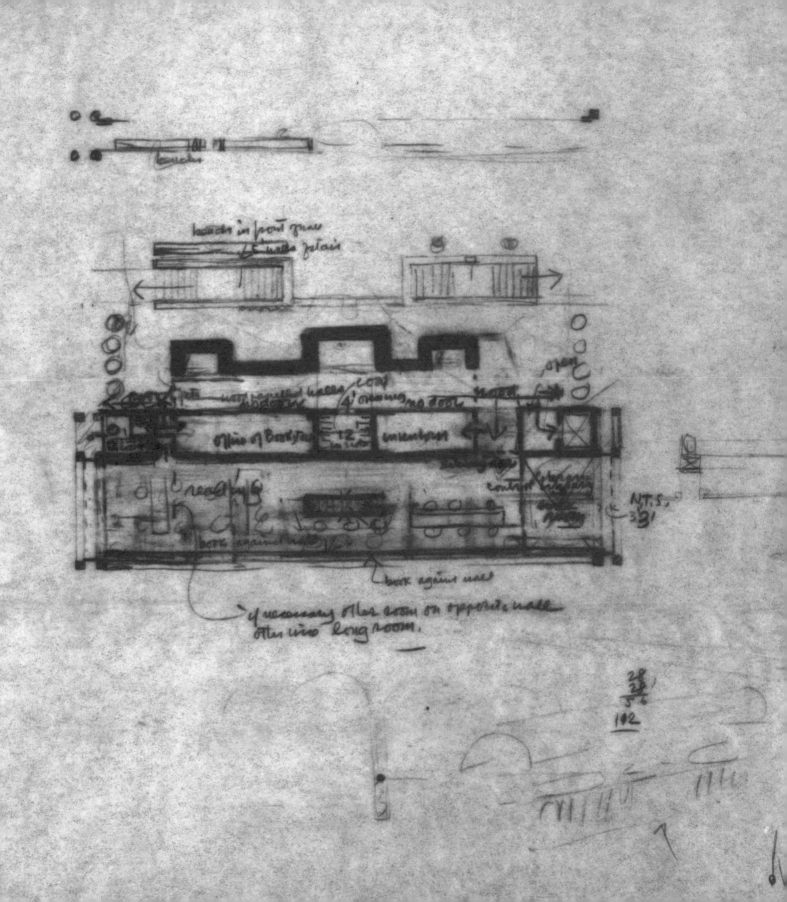

L.W

L.W
o.hit

$\frac{1}{2}$

books

books

central light —

L.W

light useo
g ovrhead light

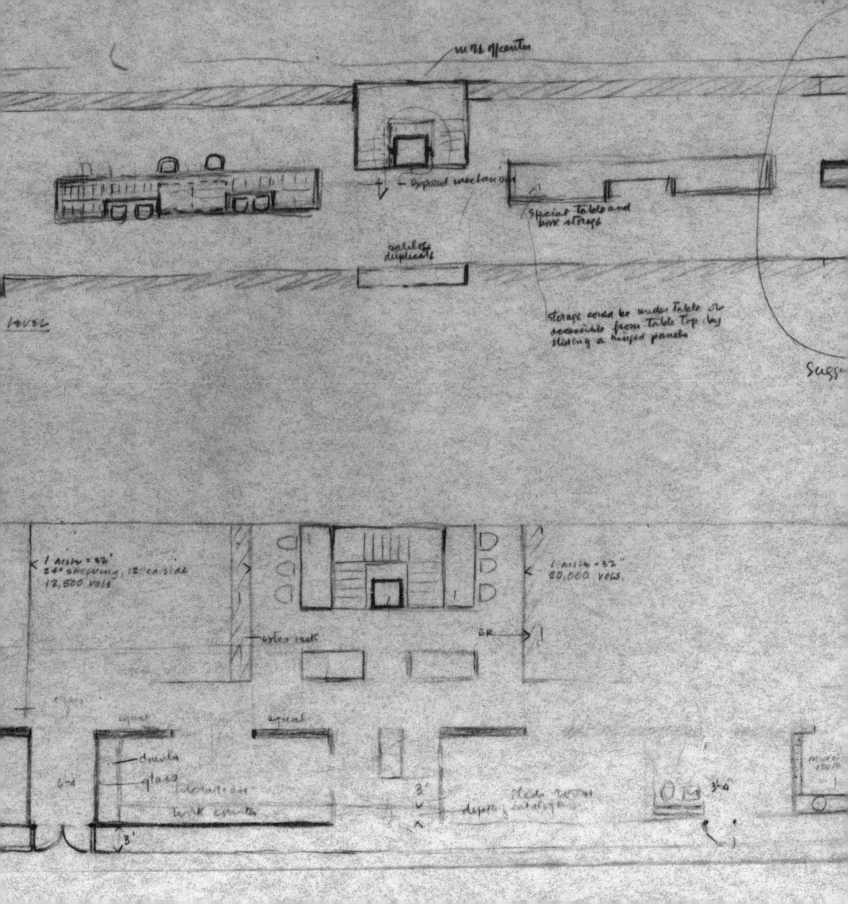

The Kimbell Art Museum Yesterday and Today: the Magic of Light

The interpretation of light in the vaults, in the exhibition halls and in the courtyards, by Michael Bodycomb

A great number of photographs of the Kimbell Art Museum have been published in the twenty-five years following its opening. We have to thank Michael Bodycomb for many of these pictures. He has been the official Museum photographer since 1986, and has taken the photographs of the museum's present appearance. We feel privileged to be able to publish his latest photographs which were taken especially for this exhibition and its catalogue.

Bodycomb goes beyond the commonplace in his sensitive photographs of the life of the building: form, light, materials, changing shadows, and art itself. Some of the photos we are presenting are unpublished, while others are well-known. This does not detract from their significance in a catalogue that accompanies an exhibition on the construction of the Kimbell Art Museum.

Twenty-five years after completion of the work the museum is practically unaltered both inside and out: all it has required so far has been routine maintenance, other than a new roof. The simplicity of the construction—which in no way equates with "simplistic" construction or architecture in this case—contributes to the ongoing preservation of the building. This is demonstrated by the color pictures that complete the illustrated part of the catalogue.

[L.B.-P.C.L.]

1.

1.
Northwest portico and reflecting pool.
2.
Southwest portico, looking down pathway
toward Lancaster Street.
3.
Detail of northwest column and corner
of vault of central portico with section of
lunette and its stainless drip molding.
4.
Detail of top of column, vault and beam,
air grill and white oak shelf in library
mezzanine.
5.
Detail showing aluminum soffit of flat
channels with air grill, concrete column,
travertine walls and lower section
of lunette.

3.4.5.

2.

6.

6.
View from lawn looking towards museum forecourt with Fernand Léger's Running Flower, 1952, at left.
7.
Museum seen at entrance to walkway from Lancaster Street.
8.
North face of the museum seen from the northwest.

8.

7.

9.
View down north side of double staircase with bookstore to left and west lobby to right.
10.
West lobby of museum, looking south.
11.
Window wall of main entrance with holly grove reflected on the glass.

9.

10.

11.

12.
View looking out the double-height,
north-facing window wall
of the conservator's studio.
13.
North courtyard with Maillol *L'aire*,
looking north.

13.

14.

14.
Winter view, looking south, from within
the north courtyard.
15.
View through doorways of connecting
staff offices beside lightwell.
16.
North gallery, as seen looking south from
a central position in the gallery.
17.
View of southwest gallery, looking north,
with fountain courtyard planted
with rose vines.
18.
South center gallery, looking south,
with installation of Asian sculpture, interior
south court yard on the right.

15.

16.

17.

18.

19.
Night view of truck dock with steel entrance door partially open.
20.
Truck dock, north side of museum, seen from the service court.

19.

Selected Bibliography

compiled by Patricia Cummings Loud

Abercrombie, Stanley. "Edison Price: His Name Is No Accident." *Architecture Plus* 1 (August 1973): 34.

Aymonino, Aldo. *Funzione e simbolo nell'architettura di Louis Kahn*. Rome: CLEAR, 1991.

Aloi, Roberto. *Musei: Architettura-Tenical*. Milan: Ulrico Hoepli, 1962.

Benedikt, Michael. *Deconstructing the Kimbell*. New York: SITES/Lumen Books, 1991.

"Bologna Arte Architettura: I Musei di Louis Kahn." *Abitare* (December 1991): 134-36.

Brawne, Michael. *Kimbell Art Museum, Louis I. Kahn*. London: Phaidon Press Ltd, 1992.

—. "Museums, Mirrors of Their Time?" *Architectural Review* 75 (February 1984): 17-19.

—. *The New Museum: Architecture and Display*. New York: Frederick A. Praeger, 1965.

Brown, Carter. "Architecture Versus the Museum." *American Institute of Architects Government Affairs Review*, Issue 71-3 (March 1971): 5-6.

Brown, Jack Perry. "Louis I. Kahn 1901-1974." In *Papers of the American Association of Architectural Biographers*, Vol. XII, Frederick D. Nichols, ed. New York and London: Garland, 1978.

—. *Louis I. Kahn: A Bibliography*. New York-London: Garland, 1987.

Brown, Richard F. "Statement: Louis I. Kahn." In *In Pursuit of Quality. Fort Worth: Kimbell Art Museum*, 1987: 328-30.

Brownlee, David B., and David G. De Long. *Louis I. Kahn: In the Realm of Architecture*. Los Angeles: Museum of Contemporary Art and New York: Rizzoli, 1991.

—. *Louis I. Kahn: Le monde de l'architecte*. Translated by Jeanne Bouniort. Paris: Edition du Centre Pompidou, 1992.

—. *Louis I. Kahn: In the Realm of Architecture*. Translated by Koyama Laboratory, University of Tokyo. Tokyo: Delphi Research Inc., 1992.

"Break-away Forms Cast Arching Roofs." *Construction Management and Economics* (April 1972): 90-92.

Burton, Joseph. "Notes from volume zero: Louis Kahn and the Language of God." *Perspecta* 20 (1983): 69-90.

Büttiker, Urs, *Louis I. Kahn. Licht und Raum. Light and Space*. Translated by David Bean. Basel, Berlin, Boston: Birkhäuser, 1993.

Cook, John W., and Heinrich Klotz. *Conversations with Architects*. New York: Frederick A. Praeger, 1973.

Cret, Paul P. "The Architect as Collaborator of the Engineer" and "Theories in Museum Planning." In *Paul Philippe Cret*, by Theophilus B. White. Philadelphia: Art Alliance Press, 1973: 16-65; 73-78.

Cuff, Dana. "Light, Rooms, and Ritual." *Design Book Review* 11 (Winter 1987): 42-47.

Davis, Douglas. "The Museum Impossible." *Museum News* 61 (June 1983): 32-37.

—. *The Museum Transformed*. New York: Abbeville Press, 1990.

Devilliers, Christian. "Louis Kahn Grande Contemporaneo." *Casabella* 55 (November 1991): 40-45, 61-62.

Domer, Dennis. "Louis I. Kahn: The Structure of Creativity." *The Structuralist* 33/34 (1993/1994): 28-34.

Filler, Martin. "America's Best Architect." *Review of The Paintings and Sketches of Louis I. Kahn*, by Jan Hochstim. *Louis I. Kahn: Writings, Lectures, Interviews*, by Alessandra Latour, ed. Louis I. Kahn: *In the Realm of Architecture*, exhibition and the book by David B. Brownlee and David G. De Long. *The Art Museums of Louis I. Kahn*, by Patricia Cummings Loud. *The New York Review of Books* (11 February 1993): 16-20.

—. "El emperador de la luz. La obra de Kahn, veinte años después." *Monografias de Arquitectura y Vivienda* 44 (1993): 22-30, 80-87.

—. "New Light on Kahn: Rediscovering the Poet of Modern Architecture." *House and Garden* 163 (August 1991): 90-95, 140.

Flanagan, Barbara. "Louis Kahn Reconsidered." *Metropolis* (December 1991): 52-6.

Frampton, Kenneth. "Louis Kahn and the French Connection." *Oppositions* 22 (Fall 1980): 21-53.

—. and Alessandra Latour. "Notes on American Architectural Education from the End of the 19th Century Until the 1970s." *Lotus International* 27 (1980-II): 5-39.

Gattamorta, Gioia, and Luca Rivalta, Andrea Savio. *Louis I. Kahn itinerari*. Rome: Officina, 1996.

Giurgola, Romaldo. "Giurgola on Kahn." *AIA Journal* 71 (August 1982): 27-35.

—. and Jaimini Mehta. *Louis I. Kahn: Architect*. Zurich: Artemis, 1975.

—. *Louis I. Kahn: Architect*. Boulder: Westview Press, 1975.

Glaeser, Ludwig. Architecture of Museums. New York: Museum of Modern Art, 1969.

Harbeson, John F. *The Study of Architectural Design*, revised edition. New York: Pencil Points Press, 1927.

Hochstim, Jan. *The Paintings and Sketches of Louis I. Kahn*. New York: Rizzoli International Publications, 1991.

Hoving, Thomas. "A Gem of a Museum." *Connoisseur* 210 (May 1982): 86-95.

—. "Money and Masterpieces." *Connoisseur* 216 (December 1986): 92-99.

"In the Philosophy of Louis Kahn, Engineering and Architecture Were Inseparable Parts of Total Form." *Architectural Record* 156 (mid-August 1974): 84-85.

In Pursuit of Quality: The Kimbell Art Museum. Fort Worth: Kimbell Art Foundation, 1987.

Ingersoll, Richard. "Louis I. Kahn: The Last Master." *Design Book Review* 21 (Summer 1991): 7-8.

Jenks, Charles. *Architecture Today*.

New York: Abrams, 1982.

Joedicke, Jurgen, and Oscar Newman, eds. *New Frontiers in Architecture*, CIAM at Otterlo. New York: Universe Books, 1961.

Johnson, Eugene J., and Michael J. Lewis. *Drawn from the Source: The Travel Sketches of Louis I. Kahn*. Cambridge, Massachusetts and London: The MIT Press, 1996.

Jordy, William. *Review of Louis I. Kahn: Complete Works, 1935-1974, by American Association of Architectural Biographies*, Vol. XII by Frederick D. Nichols, ed.

18 Years with Architect Louis I. Kahn, by August Komendant.

Louis I. Kahn, by Romaldo Giurgola and Jaimni Mehta. *Travel Sketches of Louis I. Kahn*, by Pennsylvania Academy of Fine Arts. *Light Is the Theme*, by Kimbell Art Foundation.

Louis I. Kahn: Sketches for the Kimbell Art Museum, by Kimbell Art Foundation.

The Architecture of the Yale Center for British Art, by Yale Center for British Art.

Journal of the Society of Architectural Historians 39 (March 1980): 85-89.

—. *Review of The Louis I. Kahn Archive: Personal Drawings*, by Alexander Tzonis.

Louis I. Kahn: Complete Works, 1935-74, by Heinz Ronner and Sharad Jhaveri. *Design Book Review* 21 (Summer 1991): 11-17.

—. "The Span of Kahn." *Architectural Review* 55 (June 1974): 318-42.

"Kahn's Kimbell: A Building in Praise of Nature and Light." *Interiors* 132 (March 1973): 84-91.

Kahn, Louis I. "L'Accord de l'homme et de l'architecture." *La Construction moderne* (July-August 1973): 10-21.

—. "Architecture Is the Thoughtful Making of Spaces." *Perspecta* 4 (1957): 2-3.

—. "Architecture: Silence and Light." *In On the Future of Art*. New

York: Viking Press, 1970: 21-35.

—. "Harmony Between Man and Architecture." *Design* (Bombay) 18 (March 974): 23-28.

—. "I Love Beginnings." *Architecture and Urbanism* 2 (Memorial issue, 1975): 279-86.

—. *Louis I. Kahn: Talks with Students.* Houston: Rice University, 1969.

—. "Louis I. Kahn on Beaux-Arts Training." In "The Span of Kahn," by William Jordy. *Architectural Review* 155 (June 1974): 332.

—. "Louis Kahn: Statements on Architecture." *Zodiac* 17 (January 1967): 54-57.

—. "Order in Architecture." *Perspecta* 4 (1957): 58-65.

—. "The Room, the Street and Human Agreement." *AIA Journal* 56 (September 1971): 33-34.

—. "Space and the Inspirations." *L'Architecture d'Aujourd'hui* 40 (February-March 1969): 15-16.

—. "Structure and Form." *Voice of America Forum Architecture Series*, no. 6. Washington, D.C.: Government Printing Office, [1961].

—. "The Wonder of the Natural Thing." In *Louis I. Kahn, l'uomo, il maestro*, by Alessandra Latour. Rome: Edizioni Kappa, 1986: 399-403.

Kahn-Rossi, Manuela, ed. *Museo d'arte e architettura.* Lugano: Museo Cantonale d'Arte and Milan: Edizioni Charta, 1992.

"Kahn's Museum: Interview with Richard F. Brown." *Art in America* 50 (September-October 1972): 44-48.

Koeble, Barbara L. "Kimbell Art Museum Unveils Addition Scheme by Giurgola," *Architecture* 78 (October 1989): 19.

Komendant, August. *Contemporary Concrete Structures.* New York: McGraw-Hill, 1972.

—. *18 Years with Architect Louis I. Kahn.* Englewood, N. J.: Aloray, 1975.

"The Largest Object in the Museum's Collection." *Museum News* 61 (June 1983): 38-53.

Latour, Alessandra. *Louis I. Kahn,*

l'uomo, il maestro. Rome: Edizioni Kappa, 1986.

—. ed. *Louis I. Kahn: Writings, Lectures, Interviews.* New York: Rizzoli, 1991.

Light Is the Theme. Comments by Louis Kahn, compiled by Nell Johnson. Fort Worth: Kimbell Art Foundation, 1975.

"Lighting Starts with Daylight." *Progressive Architecture* 54 (September 1973): 82-85.

Lobell, John. *Between Silence and Light: Spirit in the Architecture of Louis I. Kahn.* Boulder: Shambhala, 1979.

—. "Kahn and Venturi: An Architecture of Being-in-Context." *Artforum* 16 (February 1978): 46-52.

Loud, Patricia C. *The Art Museums of Louis I. Kahn.* Durham, North Carolina, and London: Duke University Press in association with the Duke University Museum of Art, 1989.

—. "The Critical Fortune." *Design Book Review* 11 (Winter 1987): 52-55.

—. "History of the Kimbell Art Museum." In *In Pursuit of Quality: The Kimbell Art Museum.* Fort Worth: Kimbell Art Foundation, 1987: 3-95.

—. "Kimbell Art Museum," "Yale Center for British Art," and "Yale University Art Gallery." In *Louis I. Kahn: In the Realm of Architecture,* by David B. Brownlee and David G. De Long. Los Angeles: Museum of Contemporary Art and New York: Rizzoli, 1991: 396-99, 410-13, 314-17.

—. *Louis I. Kahn. I musei.* Translated by Maurizio Romano. Milan: Electa, 1991.

"Louis I. Kahn." Architecture and Urbanism (Memorial issue, 1975).

"Louis I. Kahn." Architecture and Urbanism (special issue, 1983). The Louis I. Kahn Archives, *Personal Drawings.* Vols. 1-7. New York and London: Garland, 1987.

"Louis I. Kahn." *Monografias de Arquitectura y Vivienda* 44 (1993).

"Louis I. Kahn 1901/1974." *Rassegna.*

Anno VII, 21/1 (March 1985).

"Louis I. Kahn: Oeuvres 1963-1969." *L'Architecture d'Aujourd'hui* 40 (February-March 1969): 1-100.

"Louis I. Kahn: Silence and Light." *Architecture and Urbanism* 3 (January 1973).

Louis I. Kahn: Sketches for the Kimbell Art Museum. Fort Worth: Kimbell Art Foundation, 1978.

Louis I. Kahn. Yale University Art Gallery, New Haven, Connecticut, 1951-1953. Kimbell Art Museum, Fort Worth, Texas, 1966-1972. Edited and photographed by Yukio Futagawa, text by Marshall D. Meyers. Tokyo: A.D.A. Edita, 1976.

Lucan, Jacques. "Da Guadet a Kahn: il tema della stanza." *Domus* 50 (January/February 1986): 72-75.

Lyndon, Donlyn, and Charles W. Moore. *Chambers for a Memory Palace.* Cambridge, Massachusetts, and London: MIT Press, 1994.

McCleary, Peter. "The Kimbell Art Museum: Between Building and Architecture." *Design Book Review* 11 (Winter 1987): 48-51.

McLaughlin, Patricia. "How'm I Doing, Corbusier?" *Pennsylvania Gazette* 71 (December 1972): 18-26.

Maki, Fumihiko. "Contemporary Classic: Kimbell Art Museum." *Architecture and Urbanism* (Memorial issue, 1975): 315-21.

Maniaque, Caroline. *Louis I. Kahn, architecte.* Paris: Centre National de Documentation Pédagogique, 1992.

Meyers, Marshall D. "Louis Kahn and the Act of Drawing: Some Recollections." In *Louis I. Kahn, l'uomo, il maestro* by Alessandra Latour. First published in *Louis I. Kahn: Sketches for the Kimbell Art Museum.* Fort Worth: Kimbell Art Foundation, 1978.

—. "Marshall D. Meyers." In *Louis I. Kahn, l'uomo, il maestro,* by Alessandra Latour. Rome: Edizioni Kappa, 1986: 71-87.

—. "Masters of Light: Louis Kahn." *AIA Journal* 68

(September 1979): 60-62.

—. "Museo d'Arte Kimbell, Fort Worth, Texas (1966-72)." An interview with Marshall Meyers. *Rassegna*, Anno VII, 21/1 (March 1985): 58-68.

—. "Yale University Art Gallery and Kimbell Art Museum." In *Louis I. Kahn. Yale University Art Gallery, New Haven, Connecticut. 1951-1953. Kimbell Art Museum, Fort Worth, Texas. 1966-1972.* Tokyo: A.D.A. Edita, 1976.

"The Mind of Louis Kahn." [Interviews by William Marlin.] *Architectural Forum* 137 (July-August 1972): 42-89.

Plagens, Peter. "Louis Kahn's New Museum in Fort Worth." *Artforum* 6 (February 1968): 18-23.

Plunz, Richard A. Review of *Louis I. Kahn: L'Uomo, Il Maestro,* by Alessandra Latour. *Design Book Review* 21 (Summer 1991): 9-10.

"Post-tensioned Shells Form Museum Roof." *Engineering News Record* 187 (October 28, 1971): 24-25.

Potterton, Homan, "The Very Model of a Modern Art Museum." *Apollo* (October 1989): 264-266, 290.

Prown, Jules D. *The Architecture of the Yale Center for British Art,* second edition. New Haven: Yale University Press, 1982.

—. "Jules B. Prown." In *Louis I. Kahn, l'uomo, il maestro,* by Alessandra Latour. Rome: Edizioni Kappa, 1986: 133-43.

—. "On Being a Client." *Journal of the Society of Architectural Historians* 42 (March 1983): 11-14.

Ronner, Heinz, Alessandro Vasella, and Sharad Jhaveri. *Louis I. Kahn: Complete Works, 1935-1974.* Basel and Stuttgart: Birkhäuser, 1977.

—. and Sharad Jhaveri. *Louis I. Kahn: Complete Works, 1935-1974,* second revised and enlarged edition. Basel and Boston: Birkhäuser, 1987.

Scully, Vincent J. *Louis Kahn.* New York: George Braziller, 1962.

—. "Louis I. Kahn and the Ruins of Rome." *Quarterly of the Museum of*

Modern Art 12 (Summer 1992): 1-13.
—. "Marvelous Fountainheads: Louis I. Kahn: Travel Drawings." *Lotus International* 68 (1991): 48-63.
Searing, Helen. *New American Art Museums.* Berkeley: University of California Press, 1982.
—. *Review of The Art Museums of Louis I. Kahn*, by Patricia Cummings Loud. Journal of the Society of Architectural Historians 51 (March 1992): 109-10.
Seymour, T. S. "Contractor Challenged by Kimbell Museum Design." In *Louis I. Kahn, l'uomo, il maestro*, by Alessandra Latour. Rome: Edizioni Kappa, 1986: 321-29. First published in *Fort Worth Star-Telegram*, "The Kimbell Art Museum," special supplement (October 2, 1972).
—. "The Immeasurable Made Measurable: Building the Kimbell Art Museum." *VIA* 7 (1984): 77-86. First published in *Texas Contractor* (21 November 1972).
Shepard, Richard. "After a Six-Year Honeymoon, the Kimbell Art Museum." *Art News* 71 (October 1972): 22-31.
Smith, C. Ray. "The Great Museum Debate." *Progressive Architecture* 50 (December 1969): 84-85.
Smithson, Alison. "Review of Recent Work: Louis Kahn." *Architectural Design* 43 (1973): 530.
Speck, Lawrence W. "Evaluation: The Kimbell Museum." *AIA Journal* 71 (August 1982): 36-43.
Suisman, Doug. "The Design of the Kimbell: Variations on a Sublime Archetype." *Design Book Review* 11 (Winter 1987): 36-41.
Tor, Abba. Review of *18 Years with Architect Louis I. Kahn*, by August Komendant. *Architectural Record* 162 (mid-August 1977): 107-08.
—. "A Memoir." In *Louis I. Kahn, l'uomo, il maestro*, by Alessandra Latour. Rome: Edizioni Kappa, 1986: 121-28.
"Texas Society of Architects Twenty-five Year Award: Kimbell Museum, Fort Worth." *Texas Architect* 9/10 (1997): 78-79.
The Travel Sketches of Louis I. Kahn. Philadelphia: Pennsylvania Academy of Fine Arts, 1978.
Tyng, Alexandra. B*eginnings: Louis I. Kahn's Philosophy of Architecture.* New York: John Wiley and Sons, 1984.
Tyng, Anne Griswold. "Architecture Is My Touchstone." *Radcliffe Quarterly* 70 (September 1984): 5-9.
—. "At the AIA Bookstore: Kahn's Works, Words, Drawings." Review of *Louis I. Kahn: In the Realm of Architecture*, by David B. Brownlee and David G. De Long. *The Paintings and Sketches of Louis I. Kahn*, by Jan Hochstim. Louis I. Kahn/Writings, Lectures, Interviews, by Alessandra Latour, ed. *The Philadelphia Architect* (December 1991/January 1992): 8.
Welch, Frank D. "Condensed Poetry." *Texas Architect* 9/10 (1997): 78.
Wright, George S. "Back to Brown: Adding to the Kimbell." *Texas Architect* 3/4 (1995): 56-9.
Wurman, Richard Saul. *What Will Be Has Always Been: The Words of Louis I. Kahn.* New York: Access Press, 1986).
—. and Eugene Feldman, eds. *The Notebooks and Drawings of Louis I. Kahn.* Philadelphia: Falcon Press, 1962; Cambridge, Massachusetts: MIT Press, 1973.

Acknowledgements (Photographs and Plans)

The Architectural Archives of the University of Pennsylvania, Philadelphia
p. 8, n.3; p. 9, n. 7, 8; p. 10, n. 9, 10, 11, 12; p. 11, n. 13, 14, 15, 16; p. 18 n. 9, 10, 11, 12; p. 19, n. 13, 14, 15, 16; pp. 51, 53, 55, 57, 58, 61, 63, 65, 67, 69, 71, 73, 74, 75, 76, 77, 78, 79, 81, 83, 85, 87, 89, 91, 92, 93, 94, 95, 96, 97, 98, 99, 100, 101, 102, 115, 117, 119, 121.

Archivi del Kimbell Art Museum, Fort Worth, Texas
Kimbell Art Museum Archives, Fort Worth, Texas
p. 12, n. 3; p. 25; p. 109 n. 5, 6; p. 111 n. 12, 13; pp. 125, 127, 129, 131, 133, 135, 137, 139, 141, 143, 145, 147.

Bob Wharton (Kimbell Art Museum Archives)
p. 12 n. 1, 2, 4; p. 16, n 1, 2, 3, 4; p. 17, n. 5, 6, 7, 8; p. 28, n. 1; p. 29, n. 2, 3, 4, 5, 6, 7; p. 30, n. 8, 9; p. 31, n. 10; p. 32, n. 11; p. 33, n. 12, 13, 14; p. 34, n. 15, 16, 17; p. 35, n. 18; p. 36, n. 19, 20; p. 37, n. 21, 22; p. 38, n. 23, 24, 25; p. 39, n. 26, 27; p. 40, n. 28; p. 41, n. 29, 30, 31, 32; p. 42, n. 33; p. 43, n. 34; p. 44, n. 35; p. 45, n. 36; p. 46, n. 37, 38, 39; p. 47, n. 40; p. 104, n. 1, 2, 3, 4; p. 105, n. 1, 2, 3, 4; p. 106, n. 1, 2, 3, 4; p. 107, n. 1, 2, 3, 4.

Michael Bodycomb(Kimbell Art Museum)
p. 13, n. 5, 6, 7, 8; p. 15, n. 15, 16; p. 20, n. 20; p. 150, n.1; p. 151 n. 2, 3, 4 , 5; p. 152 n. 6; p. 153 n. 7, 8; p. 154 n. 9, 10; p. 155 n. 11; p. 156 n. 12; p. 157 n. 13; p. 158 n. 14, 15; p. 159 n. 16, 17, 18; p. 160 n. 19; p. 161 n. 20.

Marshall D. Meyers
p. 14 n. 9, 10, 11, 12; p. 15 n. 13, 14; p. 20 n. 17, 18, 19; p. 21 n. 21, 22, 23, 24; p. 22 n. 25, 26, 27, 28; p. 23 n. 29.